D1274803

THE CATHOLIC VIEWPOINT SERIES

Editor: John J. Delaney

John LaFarge, S.J.

THE CATHOLIC VIEWPOINT
ON RACE RELATIONS

———————

HANOVER HOUSE
Garden City, New York

Imprimi Potest: Thomas E. Henneberry, S.J.
Provincial, New York Province
Society of Jesus
Nihil Obstat: *John A. Goodwine, J.C.D.*
Censor Librorum
Imprimatur: ✠ *Francis Cardinal Spellman*
Archbishop of New York
June 20, 1956

Preface

During the few months elapsing since most of this book was composed in the early summer of 1955, the attention of the whole country and, indeed, of the world has been focused upon exciting events in the Southern United States. A complex web of movements for resisting and for complying with the Supreme Court's decision of May 17, 1954, unfolded during these months and at date of writing is still gathering momentum.

The reader will bear in mind, however, that regardless of the special developments in the South, the question here treated is not just regional. It is national and worldwide, and can be properly understood only when seen from that standpoint. May I say, too, that I have tried to keep the discussion from being too much bound up with events and utterances of the passing moment. It was rather my idea to gather here, in simple, convenient form, a few brief summaries of the racial situation and the principles governing it, and such practical methods as have already stood the sharp test of experience.

I wish to make special acknowledgement for the kind assistance of Messrs. George K. Hunton, Patrick J. Mullaney, and Theophilus Lewis, of the staff of *Interracial Review,* for furnishing material that I have quoted extensively; to the publishers whose material I have cited; to Rev. B. L. Masse, S.J., of the *America* staff, for reading the manuscript and suggesting improvements; and to my secretary, Mr. W. H. Dodd, of The America Press, for help with typing.

New York
Easter Sunday, 1956

JOHN LaFARGE, S.J.

5

Contents

Introduction to the Catholic Viewpoint Series

In any complex civilization, differences of opinion between various groups are inevitable. This is particularly true in a nation such as the United States, composed of peoples from all over the world, each with its own cultural heritage and background. In many cases these differences are desirable and contribute to the enrichment of our society by their very diversity. Free exchange of ideas and freedom to express one's beliefs are essential for the full functioning of the democracy we so justly cherish. Unfortunately, these differences also can result in deep cleavages which, if ignored and misunderstood, could develop into dangerous threats to the very freedoms we are all so anxious to maintain.

Where there is a large minority group with definite ideals, sometimes at variance with the customs and habits of the majority, there is always danger that misunderstanding may over-emphasize or distort the difference, unless these differences are clearly understood. Ignorance promotes dissension, whereas knowledge leads to the understanding and sympathy for the other person's viewpoint without which no democracy can long survive.

One of the fields in which ignorance can so easily lead to misunderstanding and conflict is in religion. In the United States, one of our most precious freedoms, guaranteed by the Constitution and upheld time and again by the courts, has been the freedom of religion, freedom to worship God in one's own way. Americans of all faiths are united in standing four-square in their allegiance to this fundamental tenet of our form of government.

Nevertheless, it is essential that we be constantly on the alert to maintain the freedoms so painstakingly achieved over the centuries. And no one factor can guarantee the continuance of this desirable state of affairs so effectively as an informed citizenry. Bigots and rabble-rousers fear nothing so greatly as men and women who seek information and knowledge and then apply this knowledge to the problems confronting us with intelligence and common sense.

It is the purpose of this Catholic Viewpoint Series to select various problems in which there have been misunderstandings and differences of opinion about the position of the Catholic Church. It should be noted here, however, that there are many areas of human activity in which there is no single Catholic position as such. Catholics are often to be found on opposite sides of a current controversy and as Catholics have complete freedom to do so. Catholic principles remain constant, but their application to specific conditions may and do take varied applications. Nevertheless, there are certain problems which, when approached in the light of Catholic teaching, require a particular attitude on the part of Catholics. It is mainly with this attitude that this series will be concerned.

Many aspects of the American scene are strongly tinged with a materialistic outlook. By her very nature, the Church is spiritual in her approach. She has always taught that this world is transitory and that man must bear in mind at all times the purpose of his existence. It is inevitable that there are areas where there is a definite conflict between the spiritual aims and aspirations of the Church and certain materialistic aspects of our society. This by no means implies a basic unalterable conflict between the Church and the concept of democracy as developed in America. Rather, it is the age-old conflict in men's minds which was so clearly and forcibly resolved by Christ when He said, "Render therefore to Caesar the things that are Caesar's; and to God, the things that are God's."

It is readily understandable, then, that problems have arisen when Catholic teaching is applied to situations involving the rights of human beings. Where such problems have arisen, it is most desirable that the Church's position be understood by Catholics and non-Catholics as well. Indeed, in many instances, Catholics themselves are not fully cognizant of the problem involved, its implication, and the Church's position in respect to that problem.

During the past decade, one of the most difficult problems facing Americans has been the treatment of racial minorities. The dramatic decision of the Supreme Court in 1954 revealed anew the depth and intensity of feeling toward a problem which was one of the basic causes of one of the most terrible wars of modern times. The problem is still with us and because of the Supreme Court decision is no longer quiescent but must be clearly faced and solved.

Among those for whom this is a definite problem that must be solved are Catholics. What is the Catholic position in this matter? What stand *must* the individual Catholic take? What position is the individual Catholic *allowed* to take? These are some of the aspects of this particular problem that Father La-Farge discusses in this book.

The Catholic Viewpoint on Race Relations is the first of a series of books which will examine various problems facing Catholics and the Catholic Church in the United States. Basically, the books will fit into an overall pattern. A problem will be analyzed, its historical background will be examined, the position of the Church in the matter will be stated and finally the position of the individual Catholic in relation to the problem will be discussed for his guidance. The whole purpose behind this series is to present the various problems simply but authoritatively. Each volume, by a recognized authority in the field, will be written in such a way, following, in general, the outline above, that it will be readily understandable by anyone interested in the various problems.

It is the hope of all concerned with this project that a frank and open appraisal of these problems, the situations involved, and a statement of the Church's position by recognized authorities will be of help to those seeking a genuine solution to many of these problems. The thought also is present that this series may prove of worth to many non-Catholics in explaining the position of the Church in such a manner that it will be readily understandable to one who is not Catholic.

Many times, a problem is a problem because those concerned with it are not really aware of what the problem is. By stating it simply and succinctly and by examining it in the light of Catholic teaching and principles, it is our hope that in many cases the problem will, if not disappear, at least be understood by those involved. It is the earnest belief of those preparing these volumes that if men of good will understand controverted questions and approach their solution with an open mind, in many cases the solution may become apparent. Understanding and tolerance are always the foe of bigotry and ignorance. Light always dissipates the darkness. We hope that the light generated by these books will help to dissipate the darkness of ignorance and misunderstanding.

JOHN J. DELANEY
Editor

THE CATHOLIC VIEWPOINT
ON RACE RELATIONS

PART I

The Problem of Race Relations

After the big holidays each year—such as Labor Day or the Fourth of July—the statisticians announce the total of lives lost on the nation's highways through reckless driving. The public shudders, parents warn their young, and committees ponder as to how to prevent such a waste of human life. Yet the highway casualties are trifling in comparison with the human waste caused by unresolved racial conflicts in this country. True, the clashes between racial minorities, or between minority and majority groups—such as between Negroes and white men—rarely result today in out-and-out physical violence: in cracked skulls on city streets or bodies hung from a roadside tree. The days of lynching parties are now a memory, though the memory is live enough to create an atmosphere of fear in circumstances where once there was immediate danger, and threats of violence persist in regions noted for their racial tensions. The racial hatred exhibited in connection with the death of a fourteen-year-old Negro boy, Emmett Till, in Mississippi on September 23, 1955, was a painful reminder that the roots of violence are still with us. We were again reminded when on February 3, 1956, a mob of white race fanatics came within seconds of perhaps fatal violence against a lone Negro girl student who sought to attend library classes at the University of Alabama.

Several years, however, have elapsed since the last instances of neighborhood race riots, even though the original causes of such riots are still latent and could erupt in bloodshed, were vigilance to relax. Yet, with all this relative degree of peace, the human life-waste continues: waste of manpower for the nation's progress and the nation's defense; waste of talents, which remain sterile for lack of opportunity; waste of intellectual and moral energy, so much of which must be channeled into the long and weary job of combating elementary injustices; and waste of souls for the Kingdom of God.

All this adds up to the fact that the problem of racial minorities, more than ninety years after the Emancipation Proclamation of President Abraham Lincoln on January 1, 1863, is still our country's number-one problem. It touches upon every phase of our national economy, health and security, religion and culture. Most of us do not care to discuss it, for we feel uneasily that it reveals an ugly cleavage of thought among our fellow citizens. When anyone does release a discussion, a swarm of disparate questions buzzes from every quarter.

Foreigners ask: How do you Americans justify your treatment of the Negro? Of the Oriental? Of the American Indian? How do Americans react to the Supreme Court's decision of May 17, 1954, outlawing compulsory segregation in the nation's schools?

Aggrieved Southerners inquire: Why do Northerners reproach the South, when they show as much prejudice toward Negroes or other racial groups in their own communities?

Sober citizens and employers would like to know: How can I keep my property from being depreciated by that family that wants to move in? How can I protect my children from contact with its peculiar ways? What should be my factory's employment policy? Who has the right to dictate to me whom I should or should not employ? Can Negroes fill responsible or highly technical jobs? Is it wise to train them to compete with white workers?

Parishioners are disturbed: Don't colored people really prefer to be by themselves? Aren't they really "better off" by themselves? Should we put false notions of equality into their heads? Isn't this something that the Communists specialize in? Should we "allow" them to mix in our church worship, in our church schools or parish organizations?

Do I—a Negro earnestly asks—feel I can trust the white man who suggests I co-operate with him? Isn't he always trying to get the better of me, to put me in my "place"? Should we protect injustices, or should we be satisfied with just doing the right thing, and leave the rest to God? Why are so many good and pious people indifferent, apparently, to grave injustices?

Discussion groups query: Isn't it best to leave our troubles for time to take care of, and not try to hasten the course of nature? Is the time ripe for such action? Is it overripe, and too long delayed? Is there anything I can personally do to cure racial prejudice, to lessen discrimination? Is the situation getting worse or better, and what *is* worse, and what *is* better? How do the boys in the armed forces feel about the new integration policy? And what has the Church to say about the whole affair?

These are not cooked-up questions. You hear them, in season and out of season, in countless instances where people gather to compare notes on the questions of the day, and dozens more could be added. Yet all turn upon one general topic: How can the various racial minorities in the United States live at peace with one another and with the majority group, known as the white population, in view of certain obstacles that now impede such peaceful co-existence? There are many answers to this question, contained in an immense amount of literature. The racial question may be approached from a great variety of standpoints. It enters into politics, into sociology, social ethics, history, social welfare, and religion. In this little book I am concerned with only one of these many answers: that which the Catholic Church provides. This answer is *reflective and balanced:* it is the fruit of Christianity's long experience; the converging of many conclusions drawn from the Church's age-old teaching on faith and morals. It is also *clear and unequivocal:* it tolerates no ambiguities or compromises; it exacts sacrifices where sacrifices are needed and proposes no facile cure-alls. It is sustained by official pronouncements, by a unanimity of Popes and bishops—the chief teaching and governing authorities of the Church. Yet it is not known as widely as it should be in the United States. Many of its concrete applications to human conduct have only recently been developed, and Catholic thinking on the race question has not always been as Catholic as might be desired. In very recent years, however, thanks to various movements within the Church as well as to developments in the nation itself, it has become much more widely known. The shadow-land of relative ignorance is shrinking. Finally, it is *not exclusive.* It uses the wisdom born of every variety of human experience. It permits—it urges—co-operation with each and every agency for genuine peace in our communities.

WHO ARE NEGROES?

Before propounding this answer, let's consider a few queries.

(1) Who or what is the so-called Negro minority, and where are its members located in our country?

(2) What are the principal obstacles to their living in peace together with the rest of the country?

(3) In what phases or areas of public life and of religious

life do these obstacles chiefly operate? That is to say, what is
the racial-minority problem in actuality, in the concrete?

These three points will need a bit of explanation. Here in
the United States we mean by a racial minority a general class
of persons who are commonly regarded as different from the
majority of their fellow citizens because of certain inherited
physical characteristics, such as dark skin, wooly hair, wide lips.
It is not the same, therefore, as a religious minority, such as that
of Jews or Catholics, where the difference is based upon the
profession of certain religious beliefs and practices; or a national minority, distinguished by a particular national origin:
as French, Italian, Polish, Lithuanian.

According to the United States Census Bureau, a person who
has any Negro ancestry is recorded as "Negro," even though
he is indistinguishable in appearance from "white" Americans.
The census defines as "Indian" anyone who is regarded by the
community in which he lives as "Indian." For practical pur-
poses, therefore, a person is a member of a racial minority who
is generally considered as belonging to such a specified racial
group. In many countries the expression "Negro" is identical
with what it literally says, a "black man," that is to say, a person
of purely African descent—although even among "pure" Africans there are many shades of complexion. In the United
States the words "colored" and "Negro," terms used practically
interchangeably, are applied as the Census Bureau applies
them: to all persons known to be in any way of African Negro
ancestry. Not more than twenty per cent of United States Negroes, it is estimated, are of pure African descent, and a large
proportion are as much white as Negro in their origin, many of
them much more so. But a common fate and a common desig-
nation by the white majority have welded them into a solid
minority group. The great fact that the American Negroes today are the representatives of a group who were once detribal-

ized, imported slaves, deprived of all civil and even human rights, and the experiences they have had from their fellow citizens as a consequence have ticketed them in the public mind in a way that no color accident could accomplish.

Negroes, as thus defined, are much our largest American racial minority. The figures, according to the census of 1950, are (in round numbers) as follows:

Whites 132,215,000
Negroes 14,894,000
(Roughly, 15,000,000): 9.9% of the total)
Other Non-whites 500,000
(Including Orientals)
Mexicans 2,000,000

The Negro population, according to the same census, is distributed as follows:

North 4,109,000 (27.6%)
South 10,208,000 (68.5%)
West 576,000 (1.9%)

From a religious point of view, Catholic Negroes are a minority within a minority: some 500,000 as compared with a total of 7,500,000 Negroes affiliated with one or the other of the Protestant churches, and some 7,000,000 of unchurched Negroes.

Although there are various minority groups* in the United States, each of them with its own problems of special importance, I have confined the discussion to the situation of the American Negroes.

Furthermore, in the case of the Negroes the issue is drawn with especial sharpness. They are the only part of our population who were once slaves to American citizens. Their steadfast emergence from the state of slavery, and the tensions that have

---

* There are some 600,000 Spanish-speaking people in New York City alone; by 1960, this number is expected to exceed 1,000,000.

accompanied it, have affected and continue to affect much of the social, political, and religious life of our nation.

As it is, the great body of Catholic teaching as it affects the Negroes affects also the situation of the other minority groups: racial or religious. Their problems continually overlap. With this in mind, I shall add at the close of the book a few words on the situation of the other minorities.

THE NEGRO'S PAST

To estimate the present situation of minority groups we must recall something of their past. The present situation of the Negro people in the United States reflects the experience of three great stages in their history.

The first stage was that of slavery, dating as far back as 1619, when the Dutch colonists introduced the first Negro slaves to this country.

The slavery epoch itself fell into two main divisions. In the earlier, the more or less patriarchal period of slavery, the slave's lot was bound up with the lot of the plantation and its owner, and human relationships between slave and master were more possible than in the later phase of chattel slavery. This later, chattel-slavery phase dates from the invention of the cotton gin, when the slave became a mere cog in the commercial machinery, to be ruthlessly traded and exchanged.

Emancipation inaugurated the second great stage of the American Negro's history. Theoretically, liberation from the "peculiar institution" of slavery conferred full citizenship upon the Negro, but it left his rights in society still undefined and unprotected, and his cultural condition socially deplorable. In the old slave-holding territories he soon became the victim of a new form of social control, which reproduced many of the humiliating features of the earlier slave regime. In the rest of the country he had no protection against waves of prejudice and violence. Deeply significant for the condition of the American Negro after emancipation was the contrast between his moral status in this country and that which he enjoyed under the Spanish and Portuguese regimes. In Latin America the atmosphere, with all its cruelty and abuses, made for manumission and the Church insisted upon the spiritual equality of slave and master.*

The third stage was that of rehabilitation, building up with ever-growing force from the "nadir," the utmost low point of post-Emancipation degradation around the turn of the century.

The extraordinary cultural advance of the Negro people in the United States during this period of rehabilitation leaves them none the less still facing certain serious obstacles in their struggle to live in peace with their more fortunate neighbors.

These obstacles fall pretty generally into two main categories:

(1) The first category would include ordinary human difficulties such as any people can experience, regardless of racial

---

* For extended information on this contrast, read *Slave and Citizen: the Negro in the Americas,* by Prof. Frank Tannenbaum of Columbia University (Knopf, 1947). Remarks Tannenbaum: "The attitude toward manumission is the crucial element in slavery; it implies the judgment of the moral status of the slave, and foreshadows his role in the case of freedom. Just as the favoring of manumission is perhaps the most characteristic and significant feature of the Latin-American slave system, so opposition to manumission and denial of opportunities for it are the primary aspect of slavery in the British West Indies and in the United States" (p. 69). Mentioning the condemnation of the slave trade by five Popes: Pius II, Paul III, Urban VIII, Benedict XIV and finally Gregory XVI (December 3, 1839), Dr. Tannenbaum observes: "More important in the long run than the condemnation of the slave trade proved the church's insistence that slave and master were equal in the sight of God. Whatever the formal relations between slave and master, they must both recognize their relationship to each other as moral human beings and as brothers in Christ" (p. 63).

considerations: such handicaps as poverty, ignorance, social backwardness, crime rates, poor health, epidemics, endemic illnesses, etc. Along with those physical handicaps are a multitude of cultural divergencies, arising in many instances from rough-and-ready ways of meeting the problems posed by the seamy side of life; personal manners, folk habits, etc. These can and do afflict all types of people, who have been deprived of proper health services, schools, religious training and religious facilities.

(2) They suffer other obstacles, however, precisely because of their race; obstacles rooted in race prejudice itself. In the United States large numbers of people are considered to be morally or intellectually inferior by nature, by the very reason of their particular racial ancestry. Hence, they are considered suitable for only certain types of jobs, fit to live only in certain neighborhoods, barred by their very mode of being from certain types of association with other human beings. Such attitudes are called prejudices—from the Latin *prae-judicium,* a rash *prejudgment* of a man or case—because these judgments are formed, not on the basis of carefully and impartially weighed observations, but under the influence of fixed and arbitrary standards of human measurement. People reach such prejudgments in most cases as the result of maxims and slogans inherited from former historical experiences or else, as most frequently happens, from sheer ignorance.

As a result of such basic prejudices the racial minority groups suffer from various types of *discrimination,* that is to say, they are refused the enjoyment of the opportunities for employment, self-development, or protection which are guaranteed to all other American citizens. Where these prejudices occur among religious-minded people, and even among Catholics—which, unfortunately, has been all too often the case—they have resulted in various types of *religious discrimination,* such as refusal to admit them to common worship, to an equal share in the Church's educational institutions and various kinds of organization.

SEGREGATION

Prejudice as an attitude and discrimination as a practice have fathered the notion of *racial segregation* as a means for protecting the physical and emotional comfort of the dominant white majority. Segregation is supposed to ensure social peace by the simple method of preventing any close or institutionalized association between the members of the minority and the majority groups. Used in this connection, segregation is understood as a quasi-sacred principle, accepted and fiercely defended; not just as an expedient for use in some acute emergency, as one might separate sick from well people in time of disaster. It means, primarily, compulsory segregation, the extent and area of which are determined by the majority group exclusively; a separation based precisely upon race, in the sense understood and determined by the majority group. Once accepted as a fixed social policy, segregation can be applied both in public or civic life, and in the life of religious observance, e.g., by insisting upon separate churches or separate seating places, etc. What the Church thinks about discrimination and segregation will be discussed later on; we wish here simply to determine the concepts.

THE VICIOUS CIRCLE

We have distinguished in theory between the merely general human handicaps of poverty and backwardness that racial minorities experience, in common with many members—such as the poor whites and the displaced persons and refugees—of the majority group, and the ills that afflict them specifically because of their *racial* ancestry. In point of fact, there is often little distinction between the two types. Together, they form a vicious circle. People are often prejudiced against racial minorities because of their poverty. Social retardation and ignorance have stamped on them a mark of inferiority. On the other hand, because of this same prejudice, it was extremely difficult for them to emerge from their depressed condition. After the Civil War, few cared to teach the Negroes because of their extreme backwardness, yet they remained in ignorance and poverty because so few cared to teach them.

Professor Robert MacIver shows clearly* the operation of this "vicious circle" in the Negro community. Discrimination, as he points out, leads to lower income. This in turn leads to lower living standards; hence, there will be less education. With less education, the Negro's earning capacity is lower, for he is unable to obtain good paying jobs. As a result of this lower earning capacity and the inability to get decently paying jobs, a state of frustration and resentment and inertia is set up. A young man or woman growing up in this atmosphere asks the natural question: What's the use? If I cannot obtain the type of work that will support my family, what's the use of leading a decent life? Habits of recklessness, carelessness, indifference, and re-

* *The More Perfect Union*, p. 64 (Macmillan, 1948).

sentment lead in turn to antagonism on the part of the majority of citizens, which in turn lead again to the continuance of further discrimination. And so this hopeless circle goes on spiraling ever downwards.

NEGRO PROGRESS

One of the greatest marvels of all history is the manner in which the Negroes did manage to work themselves out of this vicious circle, and achieve in a few decades a rate of progress unparalleled by any people in such numbers and in so short a time. A social revolution—in the sense of rapid social change—has taken place in the last fifteen years. Some of what has happened is the courts' doing, rather than the South's: the admission of Negroes to white graduate schools, the outlawing of the white primary election, the partial removal of segregation in interstate commerce and now, in the border states the first moves toward ending segregation in the public schools. But other changes have been purely Southern-inspired: the election or appointment to school boards in Raleigh, Atlanta, Augusta, Winston-Salem, and other cities; the stand of the major Southern churches against continued segregation; the reporting of Negro news—other than crime stories—and the use of courtesy titles for Negro women; the passing of separate lines in banks; the dropping of separate drinking fountains in some city department stores; joint use of elevators by Negroes and whites in office buildings; white taxicabs that take colored passengers; interracial union and church meetings; interracial committees to work on common civic problems.* Add to this the upgrading of Negro personnel in city police and fire departments.

* *Business Week*, December 18, 1954.

The Problem of Race Relations

Of paramount importance, too, has been the rapid advance and integration of Negroes in all the principal features of American sports, along with high prestige won by Negro athletes in the field of international contests. Particularly striking was the part played in this development by major league baseball.*

ECONOMIC PROGRESS

In the economic field American Negroes have greatly advanced in recent decades, although the progress has not been as steady and uniform as it is sometimes popularly represented. The mechanizing of the large plantations in the South made great changes in the lives of all agricultural workers and sent them during the period between the two world wars to seek employment in the cities. By the year 1950, 62 per cent of the Negroes in the United States were city dwellers.

This meant a shift to the cities and a shift to the North. In 1950, 15,000,000 Negroes were still about 10 per cent of the U.S. population, a ratio that has held constant since 1920. But

---

* "Opening the major leagues to Negro ball-players was more than a question of putting a few Negroes in the majors. It was the basic question of whether an American can support his family by working at the thing he does best on equal terms with his fellow Americans without regard to his race, color or religion" (Joe Bostic, radio announcer, ring official, and sports editor of the New York *Amsterdam News*).

"The advent of the Negro baseball player in the major leagues gave many players and fans their first opportunity to see for themselves that skin color does not determine personality or competitive ability. The baseball world has learned that essentially the Negro is the same as a white man. He has his good days and his bad days. He hurts just as badly when he is injured. He has the same feelings, problems and pleasures. The game is teaching a valuable lesson in racial integration by its acceptance of men strictly on the basis of ability" (Frank Forbes, baseball scout and member of the public-relations staff of the New York Giants).

29

whereas in 1940, 72 per cent of all Negroes were in the thirteen states traditionally classed as South, only 62 per cent—a little more than nine million people—were there in 1950. More than two and a half million Negroes born in the South were living outside of it in 1950.

The rural Negro's life, despite some fine gains in ownership and income, remained precarious. The Negro-operated farm remains a small, marginal unit whose production would be hardly missed. Though it is hard to see much future for the mass of Negroes on the farm, it has been equally hard to see much of a past. In a sense, the giant shake-out process now at work can scarcely make the Negro worse off in the next generation, though it presents terrible problems for this one.

"It is part of U.S. folklore to regard the Negro's progress as a long, straggling march that began at Emancipation and that ever since has moved the colored man slowly but steadily toward his goal of equal opportunity. The concept does no great harm; it just happens to be unprovable.

"Between 1910 and 1930, the ratio of Negroes employed in skilled and semi-skilled jobs to all Negroes employed off the farm showed only a hairline raise in the skilled class, while there was a drop in the semi-skilled group. . . . In 1941, though, this changed. Two things happened: the U.S. went to war and the Negro went to town, first physically, and then economically. And because he had so much farther to go, he traveled even farther than the whites. Under the pinch of the war's manpower shortage and the pronouncement of President Franklin D. Roosevelt's Executive Order No. 8802 on fair employment practices, the colored worker gained, and held economic ground that he had hardly penetrated before."[*]

Negro-owned business is still comparatively small; it operates

* *Business Week,* December 18, 1954.

almost entirely in a very limited sphere; it remains the exception rather than the rule. In the labor field, about one-half of Negro men and two-thirds of Negro women are still below the semi-skilled level. Against this, about one-sixth of white men and women are below it.

Officially the great labor federations are committed to full equal opportunity and condemn racial prejudice and discrimination. Both the American Federation of Labor and the Congress of Industrial Organizations issued ringing condemnations of such practices by any of their affiliates. As the recent merger of the A.F. of L. and the CIO has strengthened the Federation vis-a-vis the international affiliates, it is possible that broad official policies may have greater influence in some unions than they have had heretofore. Racial obstacles are more serious in the old-line craft unions than in the newer industrial unions.

How fast the Negro progresses economically from now on will depend partly, of course, on how fast social attitudes continue to change. But a more important factor—and a more impersonal one—will be how close the economy continues to run to full employment and how much tightness prevails in the white labor market.

Nevertheless, says *Business Week,* "the economic tide is finally running with the Negro. The only question now is how long it will take to carry him to full equal opportunity."

PROFESSION AND PRACTICE

Practically speaking, the American racial problem arises from the sharp contradiction that still exists between profession and practice in many areas of our American life, even in those larger sections of the country that are not committed either by laws or by entrenched social customs to the notion of white

31

supremacy. As a people we have made wonderful progress in this regard; the racial situation, outside of certain geographical pockets of stubborn resistance, is vastly better than it was a couple of generations ago. But we are still slow in ridding ourselves of those contradictions. Racial prejudice and its offspring, racial discrimination, still exert an influence and cause serious harm to our national welfare and to our religious integrity. A few instances may make this plain.

(1) *Education.* Our nation is committed to a policy of providing or securing adequate schooling for all its youth. We believe in equal opportunity for all, regardless of race, color, or creed. To this end we have made and continue to make immense sacrifices of money and personnel: sacrifices that grow in weight each year, with our rapidly increasing school population. Our requirements, too, become each year more exacting, as to type of buildings, school equipment, recreational and transportation facilities, etc. In the major part of the country, no distinction is made between white and non-white children in the schools: they receive, or at least are supposed to receive, equal and identical treatment throughout their courses. In such completely "integrated" school systems, individual instances of unequal treatment may occur, but they have no ultimate official sanction, so that appeal is always possible. In the seventeen states where non-white children are obliged to attend schools separate from those of the white children, gross inequalities sometimes occur: as to style of school building, length of school year, provision for school equipment, teachers' pay, etc. In many other instances, every attempt is made to carry out in the school area the principle of "separate but equal," which back in 1896 was blessed by the Supreme Court of the United States in a famous decision concerning public transportation facilities. There are many fine examples

in the Southern states of first-class educational accommodations provided for Negroes at the public expense.

Through fifty years of protest and litigation, however, the Negro minority group of the United States and many distinguished white jurists co-operating with them have contested the validity of this 1896 principle, insisting that the idea of "separate but equal" schools is by its very nature deceptive. After a series of Supreme Court pronouncements obliging several hitherto all-white universities in the segregation areas to admit Negro graduate students who otherwise could not obtain equal graduate study facilities, the court on May 17, 1954, issued a history-making decision. It repudiated once and for all the "separate-but-equal" doctrine. It held that no matter how painstaking and how sincere might be the attempt to provide equal educational facilities for the separated schools, the very fact of a compulsory separation placed a stigma upon the racial group subjected to it. This stigma of its nature did definite injury to the personality of the pupil and so defeated the purpose of the schools themselves.

The court argued directly from two obvious facts in the general social situation in the United States. These facts are quite irreconcilable. The first fact is the nation's unreserved commitment to a comprehensive program of universal educational opportunity at the public expense, open to all American youth without exception. This happens to be true especially in the thirteen states of the South where segregation laws are in force. The South ranks far below the other regions of the United States in terms of per capita income. But as a recent report of the Ford Foundation points out, it ranks well above most of the rest of the country in terms of the proportion of its income it has been spending for the education of its children in public schools. From 1940 to 1953 expenditures per pupil in Southern schools increased more than fourfold.

Some of this increased expenditure may be ascribed to the recent revolutionary changes in the economic life of the country and to the corresponding influx of people from other regions. Southern agriculture has changed in many instances from a tobacco or cotton monoculture to cattle-raising and diversified farming. Northern industrial plants have been moving in large numbers to the South.

The other obvious sociological fact lies in the psychological order. You simply cannot force young people to attend segregated schools and at the same time claim that you are offering them universal and equal opportunity. The mere fact of compulsory separation lays an evident stigma of inferiority upon the human person. This stigma inflicts a deep wound upon the personality itself. This is particularly true in a rapidly advancing and expanding democratic culture such as that of the United States. As expressed by the Supreme Court, citing a finding by another court, which nevertheless felt constrained to rule against the Negro plaintiffs:

"Segregation of white and colored children in public schools has a detrimental effect upon the colored children. The impact is greater when it has the sanction of the law; for the policy of separating the races is usually interpreted as denoting the inferiority of the Negro group.

"A sense of inferiority affects the motivation of a child to learn. Segregation with the sanction of law, therefore, has a tendency to retard the educational and mental development of Negro children and to deprive them of some of the benefits they would receive in a racially integrated school system."

This finding, they note, is "amply supported by modern authority," which they refer to in an appendix. They quote Gunnar Myrdal's *The American Dilemma* (Harper, 1944) in which the author foresaw that such a contradiction between the "American creed" of equal opportunity for all, and a practical denial—by segregation—of equal opportunity would inevitably lead to a conflict.

The reasoning of the court, therefore, turns not so much upon the wrongness *per se* of an implicitly inferior status as upon the total impossibility of reconciling such a practice with the professed public social policy of the country.

How many of us stop to reflect on the tremendous degree to which progress in the Negro community has been retarded by the substandard education so many young Negroes did receive in Southern schools in the primary and secondary grades? Poor schools, inferior teachers and poor attendance were a natural preparation for the hordes of ignorant young folk lounging on the street corners or sitting idle on the steps of the country store. In my early years of pastorate in Southern Maryland, I passed day after day a Negro public school where, at the very most, classes were held very little more than three months out of the entire school year, and little attempt was made to enforce attendance even for that minimum. So it is that many Negroes coming to the Northern cities are not fully prepared for urban living. In many parts of the South this handicap has been overcome by the better schools for Negro youth. But the effects of long, persistent tradition still remain and the present generation has the task of overcoming the negligence of the past.

Many a Negro now distinguished in educational circles tells how when he first came to the city in his youth he was obliged, even as a high school graduate, to enter sixth or seventh grade in order to make up for the deficiencies of his earlier education.

The same difficulty concerns other fields of opportunity. In the case of young women who apply for enrollment in nurse's training, no one can tell the result of repeated rejections. No one knows how many would-be nurses each year abandon the ambition or vocation of ministering to the sick and suffering.

Who are responsible for the continuance of this unjust practice of rejecting Negro aspirants for nursing diplomas? Probably, the blame must be laid at the doors of the members of hospital boards—trustees or local citizens who represent the community —who too often conform to the established local patterns of traditions of racial discrimination. This applies to communities in every section of the country, North and South. It is significant that many of these trustees and board members as fathers and mothers have chosen Negro nurses to care for their own children—in health and sickness. They would stoutly deny the charge of inconsistency. But they do not realize that their boards are maintaining barriers of exclusions which they themselves would not follow in their own homes. Hospital trustees could abolish these practices overnight.

There is, consequently, no longer a question as to what is held by the highest judicial instance in the land, but certain problems still remain.

(2) *Employment.* Let us follow the same manner of inquiry with regard to the field of employment, asking first what is the situation, then what harmful effects result from the situation and what agencies have been set on foot to correct them, and, finally, just what is the problem that confronts us precisely as Christians and Catholics.

Racial minorities complain bitterly when workers otherwise fully qualified for jobs by intelligence, skill, and character are refused employment because of their race or color. Although the area of employment open to Negro men and women is steadily enlarging, and each year sees traditional barriers broken down, there still remains far too large a backlog of employment discrimination on grounds purely of race or color, not on grounds of any other form of disqualification.

The harmful results of such an unjustly discriminating policy are patent, for it affects not only the individual discriminated against, but his family as well. It obliges, for instance, mothers of families to seek jobs outside their homes in order to support their unemployed husbands and their children. It destroys legitimate ambition, and thereby self-respect, among the youth of both sexes. And with ambition and self-respect undermined, modern youth is an easy prey to idleness, vice and crime.

The problem, therefore, is:

a) What is the moral situation of employers who claim that no public authority has a right to "dictate to them whom they should or should not employ," and consider any legislation pointed to this end as an unwarranted interference with their natural rights?

b) What position, following Catholic notions of justice and charity, should we take on types of legislation, as well as various movements for combating employment discrimination?

c) What is the moral position of trade unions which permit, or in certain cases actually prescribe, employment discrimination?

(3) *Political Rights.* Emancipation left the American Negro technically free, and supposedly endowed him with full citizenship. But the gift was illusory. Revulsion and resentment followed the brief Reconstruction period, and Negro history in the United States has been a long effort to gain in fact what he is entitled to in theory. It has been a continuous struggle against a whole panoply of civic and political inequalities, protected by a series of legal or quasi-legal devices. Such devices are: exclusion from the primary vote of the Democratic Party in the Southern states, the cumulative poll tax as a condition for voting, along with other restrictions; lack of legal and court protection against lynching and other forms of physical violence, etc. In recent years most of these major handicaps have been overcome; partly as the result of an increasingly enlightened Southern opinion, but mainly as the consequence of a series of

legal test cases brought by Negro leaders before the higher courts. For several years, lynching has ceased to be practised and is severely frowned upon in each of the Southern states, although outbreaks of intimidation and violence, including intimidation of prospective voters, have occurred in the course of the year 1955 and at the moment seem to be increasing. Mississippi, which had 32,000 registered Negro voters in 1954—out of 460,000 eligibles—had only 8,000 registered in the elections of 1955. Exclusion of Negroes from juries in criminal cases where Negroes are concerned becomes more and more infrequent, although it is still practised, as it was in the notorious Sumner, Mississippi, trial already referred to. In the nation at large, purely political inequalities are less formidable today than they were twenty or twenty-five years ago. Approximately 2,500,000 Negroes now vote in the North and West.[*]

But when issues arise that as deeply affect the Negro's political or social rights, a formidable fact remains. Those regions of the country where the Negro vote is either nullified or reduced to a minimum still exert a preponderant influence in national political affairs. They exert it either within the policy framework of their own party or else by coalition with complaisant and bargain-minded members of the opposite political alignment. This exercise of an abnormal and one-sided power has habitually blocked appeal to a majority vote in questions of legislation designed to protect certain basic minority rights.

Much of the question today turns upon the capacity and willingness of the various minority groups to use the ballot intelligently in their own behalf: a matter in which the Negroes have become, through the stress of hard circumstances, much more proficient than other, smaller minorities, such as the Indians or people of Mexican origin in the Southwest. The

[*] Simpson and Yinger, *Racial and Cultural Minorities* (New York, Harper, 1956), p. 426.

problem, precisely, is for what end—from the viewpoint of the common good—should minority citizens use their newly acquired political power. How far, for instance, should they exert their political power just in their own group interest, as narrowly conceived; how far in the interests of all?

"There is no possibility that Negroes will form a third party in the United States. Only by refusing to identify too closely with either of the major parties can Negroes use their bargaining power to advance their liberation. Negroes are interested in free participation in American life, and not in any kind of group exclusiveness."*

(4) *Housing and Neighborhoods.* The current shortage of housing presses hard upon all our citizens, regardless of racial or other social groupings. With it come various difficulties arising from the increase of congested neighborhoods. Under these crowded conditions racial or cultural differences irritate to an extent far beyond the more normal frictions felt in less congested communities. These conditions have come in the main as a sequel of major population movements, such as:

a) Migrations from the Southern to the Northern states, from the rural districts to the cities, and from Puerto Rico and other outlying localities to the mainland, and, in the more recent years, to great new industrial projects. To these add immigration from Mexico and the detribalizing of certain "liberated" Indian tribes. These movements are accompanied by an appalling increase of urban and of industrial slums, with all their sinister connotation for family life and morals and the morale of youth.

b) Expansion from the large cities into the surrounding suburban areas. Such expansion takes place as part of the natural growth of our great urban centers. It is usually accompanied by

* *Ibid.*, p. 434.

the efforts of underprivileged racial and national groups to escape from the confinement of an urban "ghetto." They wish to share with all other citizens the benefits of greater space and to enjoy more congenial surroundings in which to live and bring up their children.

The result has been the acute conflict in newer and highly improved areas between the supposed interests of the majority and the minority groups. These conflicts of interest have resulted in some cases in shocking manifestations of racial antagonism and even physical violence, such as occurred in Cicero, Illinois, and in the Trumbull Park region of Chicago. Objections to people of other races or cultures purchasing homes in sections with a homogeneous, predominantly native-white population have led to the creation of various types of restrictive agreements. Recent decisions of the Supreme Court of the United States have destroyed the legal basis of such agreements, so that they cannot be enforced by law; nevertheless, the dominant element in the community still has many ways of expressing and enforcing its position.

In some places the process has not been gradual. A certain type of real estate sale will break the usual "unwritten agreement" not to sell to Negroes. Sometimes "block-busting" real estate dealers may consciously plan a panic by suddenly introducing a non-white family into a block of homes, but this is relatively rare, however. Public auction of a house that is in tax arrears or, simply, economic pressure more commonly causes a transaction that is beyond the control of the local real estate fraternity. Through a "spite sale" an angry neighbor may seek to revenge himself on the community. This is how a panic begins.

Time and again rashes of "For Sale" signs have appeared along whole blocks of homes in Germantown or among the rows of West Philadelphia. Within a year, it will be a foregone conclusion that the block will soon be all Negro. The white owners lose confidence in their homes and their neighborhoods, and sell as quickly as possible. There are no really rational reasons why this process takes place, for the mentalities behind it are dominated by fear, pride, exasperation, and even hysteria. The whites fall prey to the folklore of intolerance and the stubborn perversity of this type of marrow-deep exasperation is something that must be witnessed to be recognized.

THE NEGRO'S PERPLEXITY

From this brief glance at some of our main trouble areas we learn that despite the phenomenal progress that the racial minorities have made in our country over the past two or three generations, despite the consequent improvement in race relations and virtual disappearance of certain peculiarly acute grievances, such as lynchings and public name-calling, there still remain certain situations where our professions of democracy and Christian brotherhood sharply contrast with the practised reality. Educational, professional, and employment opportunities are still in many respects grossly unequal. The situation of our multiplying and changing neighborhoods is day after day becoming more, not less. Behind these more evident difficulties lies a subtle, yet very tangible, factor.

The thoughtful and pious Negro finds it, as a rule, difficult to understand how it is that in the question of discrimination Catholics are supposed to conform with rigid exactitude to the prevailing social pattern. Yet, in other instances, they are enjoined to follow a bold nonconformity to current usage—in economic or family morals, in the field of education, in the observance of Friday abstinence, and so on. Holy and humble souls can absorb, as it were, this contradiction and offer it up as a holocaust to the Creator. But for the person who looks upon the Church from the outside, this same ambiguity or equivocation, this gap between Catholic teaching and Catholic practice, has long been a solid roadblock to a generalized embracing by the American Negro of the Catholic faith.

Here is the Negro's perplexity. He would like to identify himself first and foremost with the universal Church. The Church herself places no obstacle. Nor does her Supreme Pontiff nor her hierarchy create any problem, yet so many of her members continue to identify him above all other considerations—divine or human—with a mere accident of racial origin. This does not occur through positive ill will, it is true; it is the effect of a widespread and not inculpable ignorance. This, as I said, gives rise to a basic spiritual problem, the problem of a man who finds evasiveness where he is entitled to love. He is perplexed that the one Church of Christ claims his soul with absolute authority, yet at the same time so many of its members warn him not to take her teachings too universally, too seriously.

Let me once more note that these difficulties and humiliations are by no means universal. In a very considerable percentage of American Catholic parishes they are blessedly absent. In plenty of parishes or local communities Negroes, or people of any racial or national origin, are fully welcome and treated upon a fully equal and fraternal footing with everybody else; there is no question in these parishes of any kind of racial separation or discrimination. The number of such parishes is steadily growing. Some of the finest examples are right in the South, where Catholics are obliged to contend with considerable religious antagonism as well. Nevertheless, there is enough, and to spare, of the other sort of attitude scattered around the country to raise still a distressing problem. As long as such unequal treatment lasts, any individual suffers from uncertainty as to what he or she may experience in the most ordinary vicissitudes of life: ordering a meal in a restaurant, visiting a public park on a hot day, traveling on a bus, applying for a municipal position.

AMBITION AND ACHIEVEMENT

I have spoken of identification. This is a key point in the whole racial question and deserves no small attention. It must be remembered that the Negro differs in one important respect from any other of the many components of our multiform, pluralist American national community. The Negro, no matter how advanced he may be culturally or socially, remains identified by his physical appearance and physical characteristics with the once-slave group from which he originated. He carries certain outward, physical marks, which immediately set him off from the rest of men, and are the first to be noticed. Yet the Negro—outside of the aboriginal American Indian—is the only American who has no hyphen background, no traditions of a mother country across the seas. In this respect he is like the Indian, the only American who knows no other cultural tradition than the American way of life.

In this country people rise rapidly from the status of a lowly peasant to every degree of social acceptance. The social scientists call this "vertical" or "social" mobility, as distinguished from horizontal mobility, by which people move readily from one part of the country to another. We are proud, as a nation, of this trait of vertical mobility. Quite a bit of our popular literature is built upon the idea that any American, if he has the character and talent, can rise to a higher social status. The rail splitter becomes President of the United States. We like to preach the value of such mobility to our young people. We encourage their ambition. We tell them wonderful stories of achievement.

The history of the American Negro is full of such achievement, stories of heroic men and women who have risen above the handicaps of their race against incredible odds. But the Negro, even when highly educated and cultivated and the descendant of cultivated parents, is still usually looked upon as a Negro first, and as an American or citizen or neighbor only in second place. Hence the problem still remains. Where the Negro has achieved such eminence, how is he to overcome ever-clinging racial handicaps? After all, his desires differ in no way from those of other American citizens.

What, in short, does the Negro desire? One answer, simple and categorical, was given by a young Negro as follows:[*]

(1) As a human being, I want to be treated as a human being with freedom to exercise all the rights, privileges, and duties proper to a human being.

(2) As native-born American citizen, I want to be considered a first-class citizen with opportunity to enjoy all the rights and privileges and to assume all the duties enjoyed and exercised by all other American citizens.

(3) Therefore, I do not want to be set off in any special section of the country or city. I do not want special schools, churches, parks, playgrounds, restaurants, shops, etc., built and set apart especially for me. I am a law-abiding, tax-paying, native-born citizen of this country. I want all the public and semi-public institutions open to me in the same manner and in the same degree that they are open to other citizens.

(4) I do not want color to be made a determinant in any way. Of course, I have my own private social life. I do not have

[*] E. T. Lancaster, "What I, a Negro Want in America," *Interracial Review*, March, 1945, p. 391.

the slightest desire to obtrude on the social life of any other people. Nor do I wish dominance over them. I want my racial traits to set me apart from the rest of mankind only in the same manner that the traits of the Italians in America, or the Irish in America, or the French in America distinguish them from Americans of English descent. I do not want to lose my identity as a Negro. If a miracle could be performed and I was changed over night into a member of some other race, I think it would be a calamity. But I do not want the fact that I am a Negro to set me apart for special treatment.

(5) I do not want to see the institutions and businesses closed which the Negroes in America have worked and sacrificed to establish. I take particular pride in the institutions and businesses owned and operated by ourselves. I would like to see more of them, better organized, better supported, serving the whole community without regard to color.

(6) But the Negro people cannot ask for equality and special help (more than is given to other similar groups) in the same breath. If colored Americans ask white Americans to help them create special institutions to serve only their [colored] needs, that is segregation—call it what you will.

(7) As to miscegenation—that fear is ridiculous. The majority of Negroes prefer to marry their own. Marriage means a mutual consent, and cannot be forced upon anyone. Laws against legal marriage have not stopped miscegenation. Advocating intermarriage will not make it more frequent.

(8) Discrimination is not so much the result of prejudice, but prejudice is the result of discrimination. Segregation feeds prejudice and keeps it alive; and it would be just as bad if we Negroes were the dominant group and the white people the victims. Lack of friendly contact breeds suspicion, distrust, violence, fear.

(9) The objective to work and pray for:

Destruction of all segregation.

Equal opportunity to use whatever talents God has given each individual.

Real freedom under the law for all citizens, white and colored alike.

Then leadership and social relations will take care of themselves.

The following brief summary, from a letter addressed to an inquiring Catholic social worker, may prove helpful:

"Your letter asking for further information about the interracial problem is very encouraging. Your very evident interest in this question leads me to explain why this problem should be of particular interest to those who are preparing to enter the profession of social service.

"First, we have that which is approximately called the *interracial* problem. This has to do with race relations; the establishment of interracial justice, interracial understanding, interracial co-operation, the recognition of rights and securing opportunities—economic, industrial, social, and educational—that have too long been denied to the Negro in America.

"The second aspect of the American race problem is that which has to do with the interior progress of the Negro group. This is primarily a *racial* problem, as it has to do with the progress of individual Negroes and of the race itself. The program to be applied is educational. It involves the development of a proper initiative, and encouraging the spirit of industry and ambition. In this particular undertaking the leadership and direction must come from the intellectual leaders of the race. This does not mean that the white group should not participate. They can and should co-operate wholeheartedly, but the responsibility is very properly that of Negro leaders, who recognize it as an important racial undertaking. We must not forget, however, that only a few of the more highly educated Negroes are engaged in this endeavor. This is due to the fact that so much time and effort are necessarily devoted to the fundamental problem of securing social justice for the Negro. As long as they are obliged to confine their efforts to the task of achieving the fundamental rights and privileges that are properly theirs as men and as citizens, just so long will there remain a definite cultural lag among the majority of Negroes. Today we find that individual and racial progress are hampered because of the fact that the Negro must first of all obtain the fundamental rights and opportunities that are essential to the security and welfare of the race."

THE CATHOLIC POSITION

What is our attitude, as Catholics, toward the idea of racial segregation itself? Is this in accord with Catholic teaching, with our doctrines on the matter of charity and justice? Can we, as Catholics, endorse the idea of segregation in the matter of schools, in the area of public transportation or public recreation, in publicly maintained institutions such as hospitals?

In particular, how do we stand in the matter of our own Catholic schools, and what, if any, steps have they taken in this regard?

The same query would apply to our Catholic hospitals and nursing schools, and to various types of charitable institutions.

As I said at the beginning, there is a Catholic doctrinal answer to those who query about our principles; there is a stimulating *factual* answer to give to those who wish to scrutinize our Catholic record. But it is important that the answers be exact, and not such as shoot wide of the mark.

Moreover, even when the schools have been "desegregated,"

that is to say, when pupils of another racial group have been admitted to study under equal conditions with those of the majority group, there still remains the question of integration in the full sense of the word. The same could apply to the desegregation of hospitals and other public institutions. We wish to know what is our Catholic attitude toward the problem of integration. How far does our faith encourage it? What aids does the Church offer towards its accomplishment?

In the following chapters we consider the nature of the *ideal* which we propose as the answer to the problem, and the various *ways* in which we may help to translate this answer into reality.

PART II

The Catholic Position: The Record

As to the Catholic viewpoint on these problems, we need to keep two concrete facts in mind. First, the Catholic Church has—absolutely speaking—a long record of working for the spiritual and cultural welfare of the various minority groups in this country, and particularly for the Negroes. It is a record, in countless instances, of wonderful devotion, amazing initiative and heroic sacrifice. Nobody can chart a navigable course for the present without consulting the routes traveled over in the past. Great effort and great personal sacrifices have been made by many priests and various religious communities, and by some very charitable lay people, to supply the Negroes with the Church's ordinary ministrations: her worship, sacraments, preaching, and pastoral care; her schools and charitable institutions; her various types of parish organization; her opportunities for religious and priestly vocations. I have said "absolutely speaking," for the record as to what *has been done* is full of glorious and inspiring examples, viewed from any angle. The record falls short rather in what was *not* done by American Catholics as a whole: the many years that elapsed before any organized work for the American Negroes was set up; the scanty support, financial and moral, such work received. The apostolate in its earlier years did simplify the issue and—

whether through harsh necessity or not—avoided tackling some of the most difficult issues of human dignity and human rights.

In recent times the Catholic Church in the United States is no longer satisfied with the former limited approach. It aims to minister to the *total man:* the inhabitant of both worlds and both communities, the spiritual and the temporal; the individual and the member of the family; the Catholic and the citizen; the parishioner and the voter.

THE PROTESTANT RECORD

As the author has noted on various occasions, the religious influence of Protestantism was an important factor in the spectacular advance of the American Negro. Protestantism is bound up with the Negro cultural tradition. The spirituals, the American Negro folk-music, originated in Protestant Evangelistic worship, which encouraged full popular self-expression. They were first publicized by the Fisk University Jubilee Singers, a Protestant church organization. Until Xavier University in New Orleans developed its superb all-Negro mixed choir, the great Negro choral groups were usually affiliated to some Protestant institution.

With rare exceptions, the great heroes of Negro history in the United States were Protestant: educational geniuses, such as Booker T. Washington, George Washington Carver, and John Hope Franklin; liberators, like Frederick Douglass, Sojourner Truth, and Harriet Tubman; poets, authors, statesmen, inventors. The white leaders in the great anti-slavery movement that led to Negro emancipation in 1863 were Protestant abolitionists, while the Catholics failed to follow the lead of Daniel O'Connell, in Ireland, and John Boyle O'Reilly, the great Irish patriot, in this country, and sided with the slave-owning South in that mighty struggle. (There were powerful historic reasons for this turn of Catholic sentiment, one of them being the bitter, fanatical anti-Catholic and anti-foreign attitude of so many of the abolitionist leaders.) Protestant preachers and writers defined in strong and biblical terms the central moral problem involved in the Civil War.

Scholars like Tannenbaum (cf. p. 24) emphasize the Negro's very different situation in Latin America. The slave in the Catholic culture of the Spanish and Portuguese dominions enjoyed a moral status, as a human being and as a prospective citizen, which he did not enjoy under his Anglo-Saxon masters. None the less, most of the movements in this country to combat the existing social pattern were of Protestant, not of Catholic, inspiration.

With all their imperfections and compromises in handling the racial problem, the major Protestant denominations in the United States deserve a lasting credit for instructing vast numbers of the American Negro people in certain basic doctrines of Christianity. They gave them the hope of the Scriptures and the knowledge of the Saviour as well as the sacrament of baptism; they sustained their spirits in times of dire affliction and trained them in educational and in some cases social and political leadership. Finally, especially in later years, the various Protestant national religious organizations, including the Quakers, developed a galaxy of men and women from among their white membership dedicated to the work of promoting better race relations.

Protestantism's weakness as a social force lay in its lack of any central spiritual authority. This laid it open to numberless divisions and schisms as well as to passivity in the face of lay church leaders whenever they were determined to maintain a rigid pattern of white supremacy. Negro Protestantism would naturally reflect the atmosphere of the epoch for better or worse. Present-day stress on social benefits and social activities is paralleled by a corresponding increase of such activities in the more "progressive" Negro denominations. The prevailing atmosphere of secularism and of contempt for higher supernatural motives is paralleled, according to reports of various Protestant church bodies, by a corresponding impatience of Negro youth with the other-worldly philosophy that so moved the older generation.

Hence it is that the Negro who has been a member of a local Protestant church gives up certain very tangible advantages on leaving his own church to become a Catholic. Ostracized in great measure already by the white community, he finds himself now ostracized by persons of his own race. On the other hand, he does not always find himself cordially received by the Catholic white church community of which he is theoretically a member; in fact, there are instances in which he may encounter distinct hostility on the part of both clergy and laity unless he keeps strictly to the fellowship of his own people.

CATHOLIC MISSIONS

The record of the Catholic Church's work on behalf of the Negro people in the United States must be weighed against the immense difficulties that slavery and emancipation bequeathed to our country and to the tiny minority of Negro Catholics: only about 100,000 of the seven million Negroes who lived in the United States in 1863. Concerning the Church's fundamental concern for the Negro's spiritual welfare, there has been no uncertainty; but any effective work was terribly handicapped by the ruined condition of the South after the war, in which the Church naturally shared; by the intense bitterness that economic competition caused between the Negroes and the Catholic Irish in the Northern cities. Added to these factors was the preoccupation of American Catholics for the various national-origin groups; the separate language parishes, the national organizations, etc.

No sooner was the war over than Baltimore's Archbishop Martin John Spalding convened in 1866 the Second Plenary Council of Baltimore, and declared to the assembled bishops: "I think it is our urgent duty to discuss the future status of the Negro. . . . We have a golden opportunity to reap a harvest of souls, which, neglected, may not return," and this attitude was endorsed by Rome. When the Third Plenary Council of Baltimore convened in 1884 it recognized the inability of the Southern bishops to cope with the problem that the Second Plenary Council had handed on to them, and formed a "Commission for Catholic Missions among the Colored People and Indians." Progress, however, remained slow, and in 1907 the archbishops and bishops of the United States formed the Catholic Board for Mission Work among the Colored People, whose first director general was the late Monsignor John E. Burke, of New York City. The board initiated an annual collection for the Negro and Indian missions, but the amount contributed remained for many years pitifully small, and has never, in fact, been worthy of the cause it represents, whether the Negroes or the Indians are concerned. At the death of the great Franciscan missionary among the Navaho Indians, Father Anselm Weber, O.F.M., his biographer, Father Robert Wilken, O.F.M., quoted a Franciscan friend as saying that "the friars would easily have won over the whole second generation of Navaho in the St. Michael's, Arizona, mission shed if the mission had been properly financed."[*]

* Anselm Weber, O.F.M., *Missionary to the Navaho* (Milwaukee, Bruce, 1955), a scholarly work packed with information on the missions and the problems of the American Indian.

Already, from the first half of the eighteenth century on, the Church had a fine record in certain localities for the amelioration of the social and moral condition of the slaves, as among the old Jesuit missions of Maryland, Louisiana, and Missouri. This work the American Jesuits have never discontinued. The Jesuit "mother-parishes" of Negro Catholicity, many of them rural, have traditionally been the root source of Catholic faith and piety for the newer Negro Catholic communities in such cities as Baltimore, Washington, Philadelphia, St. Louis, Chicago, and New Orleans.

But there was no organized effort to win the souls of the American Negroes after the Civil War until, in 1871, the priests of the St. Joseph's Society, or the Josephite Fathers as they are commonly called, began their work for the Negroes in this country. Father Herbert Vaughan, later Cardinal, began the Society in 1866, at Mill Hill, near London. In obedience to the wish of Pope Pius XI, and in response to the plea of the American bishops, Father Vaughan brought four priests of his missionary congregation to Baltimore. In 1893 they set up an independent foundation with headquarters at Baltimore. From there, for the last sixty-two years, they have been going out to cities, small towns, and rural districts all over the South, bearing, in the words of one of their number, "the heats and burdens of a prejudiced day," creating parishes and schools out of nothing at all in the way of resources, existing Catholic faithful or previous outside aid.*

Three years after the Josephites, the Fathers of the Holy Ghost took up Negro mission work, and with the Josephites were its backbone until they were joined by the Divine Word

---

* The Josephites' illustrated monthly publication, *The Colored Harvest* (1130 North Calvert St., Baltimore 2, Maryland. $1.00 a year), enables its readers to keep in touch with front-line missionary work in the Negro field.

Missionaries in 1906 and the (Lyons, France) African Mission Fathers in 1907. Other missionary organizations, both religious orders and diocesan, have since then taken over assignments on behalf of the Negro. Side by side with these various agencies was the quiet, hidden growth of the colored sisterhoods of our country: the Oblate Sisters of Providence, founded in Baltimore in 1829; the Sisters of the Holy Family, established in New Orleans in 1843; and the Franciscan Handmaids of Mary, a smaller group who began in New York City in 1916.

On March 3, 1955, a solemn pontifical funeral Mass celebrated by the Archbishop of Philadelphia, Most Rev. John F. O'Hara, C.S.C., marked what was probably the greatest tribute ever paid to any American woman by the Catholic Church of the United States: Mother M. Katharine Drexel, foundress in 1891 of the Sisters of the Blessed Sacrament for Indians and Colored Peoples. Along with her sister Louise, the late Mrs. Edward V. Morrell, of Torresdale, Pennsylvania—who joined with her in her innumerable benefactions—she was heiress of the income of an immense fortune. Mother Katharine initiated and supported a far-reaching system of educational institutions for both Indian and Negro youth, ranging from rural grade schools through vocational training schools to Xavier University in New Orleans, the first and only Catholic university for Negroes in the United States.

These are but few of the most prominent items in a list which, to be complete, would need to include such outstanding undertakings as the educational and social welfare center, the City of St. Jude, near Montgomery, Alabama, initiated by the late Rev. Harold Purcell; the comprehensive mission community of the Fathers of the Most Holy Trinity in Mississippi; and many others in more recent times.

NEGRO CLERGY

Though many dioceses now train colored candidates for the priesthood, the only major seminary in the country established exclusively for them is St. Augustine's at Bay St. Louis, Mississippi, which saw its first graduates ordained in 1934, and which has since sent out more than thirty other priests. The seminary is in charge of the Divine Word Missionaries (S.V. D.), in its origin a German community, with missions in Africa, Southeast Asia, and elsewhere around the world. St. Augustine's is now conducted on an interracial basis, accepting all candidates for the missionaries' community who are of Southern origin, whether white or colored.

The attitude of all these communities toward the Negroes is that of the Venerable Francis Libermann, the Jewish convert who founded the Fathers of the Holy Ghost: "Perfect them, sanctify them . . . and make them, slowly and surely, into a people of God."

That this country has now at last a growing Negro Catholic clergy rich in promise of learning and holiness is attributable in a paramount sense to the long, patient educational labors of the Divine Word Missionaries. The incident that took place on October 2, 1955, in the archdiocese of New Orleans, to which we refer later on pages 101–102 called the whole world's sudden attention, as with a flash of lightning, to what the Divine Word Missionaries really stood for, and the nobility of what they have already accomplished. For the day-by-day story of their work, consult their fine monthly publication, *The Saint Augustine's Messenger*, published at Bay St. Louis, Mississippi.

OBSTACLES TO MISSION WORK

Three spiritual hardships have been the habitual companions of the missionaries to the Negro in this country.

The first of these has been the apathy and indifference shown to the work by the public in general and even by the missionary's fellow Catholics. In many cases people have visited upon the person of the missionary the prejudice they felt against the Negro himself.

The second of these hardships has been one much more difficult to bear than the former. Many a missionary who is perfectly satisfied with suffering himself the dislike, contempt, or indifference of his fellow Catholics has had his heart torn asunder on seeing the fruit of his work frustrated by prejudice and discrimination against his flock. He has known and foreseen the evil effects of such discrimination in the future of the children, the boys and girls whom he has labored to educate. Sisters and Brothers have trained Negro young people, knowing with a heavy heart that these will have to face the hostile world once their training is completed. They have seen young men and women of virtue and talent refused an opportunity because of their race and color.

A still more trying suffering has awaited the priests and nuns engaged in this work. In many instances, they have found themselves obliged to conform to a social pattern which their own Christian conscience and their own sense of inner decency reject. If they wished to reach their people and do anything for them, they have had to put up with a pattern of segregation, to try to adapt themselves to an unjust and mechanical pattern of human relationships, outworn as a civic policy and contrary to the spirit of Catholicism as a policy of the Church.

The joy of the harvest from the Church's work for the colored is so great, its fruit so abundant, its glory so splendid, that it makes up amply for all the hardships and humiliations and deprivations that have gone into the task. The missionary finds the wonders of God's mercy revealed in the people whose lot he shares. It is an immense consolation for those splendid men and women, white and black, who are devoted to the spiritual welfare and the educational welfare of the Negro in this country to see the vast fruit that has been obtained in spite of the heavy conditions under which they have had to labor.

The very nature of the mission work, however, brought into prominence the peculiar difficulties which beset the racial minorities in this country. No matter how painstaking was the spiritual care of the colored people, no matter how much energy was expended upon the education of their youth, the work was in great measure frustrated by the indifference shown toward the Church's apostolate to the Negroes by Catholics themselves. Even where downright hostility was absent, mission work for the colored people languished from a general apathy. Those who devoted their lives to the Negroes' welfare did a job which for the most part made little or no appeal to the average American Catholic's sympathy or understanding. Moreover, the tremendous migration from the rural districts to the cities, and from the South to the North, especially after World War I, created new and special racial tensions. Negro Catholics found themselves strangers in their new surroundings.

Parish priests and educators were distressed at finding the products of their schools discriminated against when the young people applied for jobs or for higher professional training.

NEGRO CATHOLIC INITIATIVE

At the same time, Negro Catholics became increasingly discontented with their situation in the Church itself. The separate parish church and school system, deliberately adopted by the missionaries as a hopeful "way out" from the difficulties and indignities their black charges suffered in the "white" parishes, became themselves a source of dissatisfaction to the Catholic Negroes. As they advanced in education, and as they became conscious of the improved status enjoyed by the various national groups in the United States, they became more and more dissatisfied with being relegated to separate arrangements in biracial churches; or else to separate churches, schools, organizations, to exclusion from hospitals, etc., and thus in general from the normal life of the Catholic Church in America. There was also an increasing demand for a Negro clergy.

As a result, an organized protest movement took place, under the auspices of the Federated Colored Catholics of America. This organization had its first humble beginnings in the early 1920's among the colored Catholics in the rural congregations of St. Mary's and Charles Counties, Maryland, at the instigation of the late Rev. Abraham J. Emerick, S.J. It was then amplified into a federation of the various societies in the scattered colored mission parishes around the whole nation. Under the guidance of its president, Dr. Thomas W. Turner, professor of plant biology at Hampton Institute, Virginia, the Federated Colored Catholics grew in numbers and prestige, and held important rallies in the various large cities of the country.

For the first time in their history, the colored Catholics of the United States became conscious of one another as being a distinct and in many ways an important group within the

Church in America. Correspondence, exchange of ideas and visits were arranged between people in the older rural parishes and those who had emigrated to the city, and between the various urban Catholic communities around the country. They exchanged information, and took note of their assets as well as of their liabilities. Their annual gatherings brought their existence to the notice of the general public, outside the Church as well as within it. Their impressive and dignified conventions, held under the auspices of the local Church authorities, attracted the interest and co-operation of the bishops and of many of the clergy who were not engaged in the Negro apostolate. In connection with their conventions, they assembled for worship outside the limits of the predominantly or all-Negro neighborhood. A magnificent solemn pontifical Mass celebrated on September 3, 1932, by His Eminence, Patrick Cardinal Hayes, in St. Patrick's Cathedral in New York, and attended by delegates from all over the nation, was the most impressive single event that had ever occurred in the history of the Catholic Negroes of the United States.

The Federated Colored Catholics, in a word, definitely registered the Negro upon the great chart of American Catholicism. The organization created an added pride in lay participation in the Church's life, and clearly formulated at its sixth annual convention in Detroit, September, 1930, the basic aspirations of Negro Catholics under the title "Catholic Justice": *

"We wish to earn a decent livelihood; free from interference based upon merely racial attitudes.

"We desire to educate all our boys and girls in Catholic schools, from the primary school to the university, according to each one's native ability.

"We desire admission to Catholic institutions, where the de-

* *Interracial Review,* May, 1934, p. 59.

nial of such admission involves the loss of tangible goods, to which, as Catholics and human beings, we may legitimately lay claim.

"We wish as Catholics to insist on the sacredness of human life. We condemn every violation of law in the taking of life, no matter what the crime.

"We wish to enjoy the full rights of citizenship, in direct proportion to the duties and sacrifices expected of our group, and cheerfully rendered by us to our country in peace and in war.

"We wish all our fellow citizens, without exception, to be freed from the obsession that Negroes' progress is harmful to American civilization; and to recognize in word and deed that ours is a common cause; that the good of one group is the good of all.

"We do not wish to be treated as 'a problem,' but as a multitude of human beings, sharing a common destiny and the common privilege of the Redemption with all mankind."

PROBLEMS OF THE FEDERATION

Impressive, however, as were these occasional demonstrations, certain basic weaknesses prevented the Federated Colored Catholics from achieving the result they professedly set out to accomplish: that of obtaining for the Negro a full and equal status in the life of the Catholic Church in this country. Impressed by the supposed power of the various national-origin or national-language groups in the American Church, such as the German Central Verein, the Ancient Order of Hibernians, the various Polish, Lithuanian, Italian and French-Canadian societies, the leaders of the Federated Colored Catholics relied strongly upon the hope of bringing a respectful and filial, but unified, mass pressure to bear upon the Church in order to obtain recognition of their rights. But the analogy was weak. The Negroes had no ties with the Old World, no hyphens, to strengthen them. The importance of all these various national groups, such as it was, decreased rapidly at the turn of the century, and still more rapidly after World War I. Year after year, at the Federation's conventions, eloquent speakers renewed their demands for recognition and protested against manifest injustices and discriminations. Church authorities, high and low, were repeatedly called upon for redress. But the tone remained one of demand, and the more repeatedly the demands were uttered, the less attention and interest did they create. As one prominent member of the organization commented: "We spent a great deal of money, time and energy talking *about* people whom we should have been talking *to*." In spite of good intentions, the net effect of Negro solidarity proved to be a tremendous obstacle to integration in Catholic life. A separatist organization was not in a very strategic position to protest against separatism.

A NEW APPROACH

The bold initiative of the Federated Colored Catholics did, however, clear the way for a new approach to the problem of the Negro's status in the Catholic Church and the attitude of Catholics toward his status in the nation as a whole. In connection with the Federation's activities, the clergy in various parts of the United States who were engaged in work among the colored people had become better acquainted. So they pooled their efforts to create a more sympathetic attitude toward the colored people and toward work for the colored among the rest of the clergy and the Catholic people of the United States. Under the title of the Clergy Conference on Negro Welfare, meetings were held over a number of years in the Northeastern area. This led to similar clergy conferences in the South and particularly—and very effectively—in the Midwest. Discussions led to a study of the chief racial problems, and various projects were designed in order to make the Catholic clergy of the United States, in the words of one of the Conference's most active members (the late Father Cornelius J. Ahern, of the Archdiocese of Newark, N.J.), "colored conscious."

Devices were studied as to how to spread a better understanding of Christian principles on race relations among the public at large. With regard to the specific problems of the educational field, the Catholic Students' Mission Crusade, with headquarters in Cincinnati, Ohio, did much to create a more liberal and friendly attitude toward the Negroes and other racial minorities in Catholic educational institutions. The strong stand taken by several leading colleges and universities against any form of racial exclusion or segregation also helped greatly to set the current in a new direction.

THE COLLEGES LEAD

Outstanding in this respect was the College of the Sacred Heart, Manhattanville—then located in New York City, now at Purchase, N.Y.—under the leadership of its former president, the late Mother Grace Dammann, R.S.C.J.

A group of twelve students at Manhattanville decided to look into the matter and see what they could do of themselves. All they needed was to glance around the college on Convent Avenue or down West 133rd Street to sense the grounds for taking possible action. They consulted, accordingly, with a small group of New York Catholic laymen and with their assistance drew up, in January, 1933, a project of resolutions. These they submitted to the entire student body for appraisal and discussion. Making no noise outside the college walls, but causing a very lively debate within, the project was thrashed out from every point of view. Finally, at a meeting of the college's Catholic Action Forum, held on May 3, 1933, the following resolutions were adopted. They have been known ever since as the Manhattanville Resolutions.

"Whereas I am enjoying the privilege of a Catholic higher education, I recognize that I have certain duties and obligations toward my fellow man, among which I must consider my conduct and attitude toward the American Negro.

"I therefore resolve to carry out and adhere to the following resolutions:

"1. To maintain that the Negro as a human being and as a citizen is entitled to the rights of life, liberty, and pursuit of happiness and to the essential opportunities of life and the full measure of social justice.

"2. To be courteous and kind to every colored person, remembering the heavy yoke of injustice and discrimination he is bearing. To remember that no race or group in America has endured the many handicaps that are his today.

"3. To say a kind word for him on every proper occasion.

"4. Not to speak slightingly or use nicknames which tend to humiliate, offend, or discourage him.

"5. To remember that the Catholic Church and the Catholic program of social justice have been called 'the greatest hope of the colored race.'

"6. To recognize that the Negro shares my membership in the Mystical Body of Christ and the privileges that flow therefrom and to conduct myself in accordance therewith.

"7. To give liberally on the Sundays of the year when the

collections are devoted to the heroic missionaries laboring among the Negro group.

"8. To become increasingly interested in the welfare of the Negro; to engage actively in some form of Catholic Action looking to the betterment of his condition, spiritually and materially."

The action of the Manhattanville students met with an immediate and enthusiastic response. *America*, the national Catholic weekly review, commented June 10, 1933, as follows:

"If the spirit in which these noble resolutions were conceived becomes prevalent among the younger generations of Catholics in this country, the most difficult of America's human problems will be solved. Best of all, it will be solved on the only lasting basis, that of true social justice. In this day of new deals, it becomes Catholic youth to be in the vanguard to see that all our fellow citizens share in them."

Manhattanville's prominence in the interracial movement, originating from Mother Dammann's initiative, persisted in the following years. After her death it continued under the leadership of her brilliant and zealous successor, Mother Eleanor O'Byrne, herself a native of Georgia. Its most important development lay in the work of organizing the interracial activities of the Catholic colleges and universities throughout the country, through the Commission on Interracial Justice of the National Federation of Catholic College Students.

The National Federation of Catholic College Students was founded in 1937, and deals with special-interest fields and vital problems through a federated commission system. All Catholic college students, on any campus in the United States, are able to participate in a program of action outlined by one of the national commissions.*

* "Throughout the world, student organizations are the training grounds for the leaders of national opinion. They play an important and some-

The National Commission on Interracial Justice came into being in 1944 and was established at Manhattanville College. Principal activities of the Commission are: providing programs of action, literature and aid to regional and local interracial units; sponsoring annual poster and literary contests; publishing the *Interracial Quarterly;* securing funds for Negro scholarships, and encouraging the celebration of an annual interracial week in Catholic colleges throughout the nation which is the high point of their program for the year.

The student awakening was not confined to the North. Significant was the following declaration by a group of Southern collegians adopted in 1951:

"We must accept the fact that the doctrine of the Mystical Body applies here and now in the South. Can we continue to say that the encyclical on the Mystical Body 'is all right for Europe where things are different. It doesn't apply to us. The Pope didn't understand us. We're living in the South—in a white society. Anybody with sense knows that.'

"There is no doubt that in the South people and situations are different. Certainly our day-by-day approach to integration in the Mystical Body cannot follow some Northern or Western plan. It has to be based on the facts here. Our plans must be built on the present social situation which is changing rapidly.

---

times decisive role in the political destiny of many countries. Communists, recognizing this fact, are engaged in a world-wide program to penetrate student organizations.

"The attitudes and actions of Catholics in America have a bearing on the course of student opinion abroad. The way we comport ourselves in the United States is a matter of immediate and lasting interest throughout the world.

"The program of the National Federation of Catholic College Students to further racial understanding in the United States is an encouragement and assistance to the Catholic students of South Africa in their efforts to counteract communist exploitation of the racial situation among students in that country" (John Simons, Director of Student Activities, Foundation for Youth and Student Affairs).

Even in the South there are marked differences between one city and another, between urban and rural areas.

"In spite of all this, we cannot cast aside the profound teachings of the Holy Father. It is only too easy to suggest that ecclesiastical authorities should stick to sermons on making pilgrimages and anti-communist propaganda. Although there are a lot of things we college students do not know, we are certain of two things. First, the Mystical Body of Christ is not an impractical pipe dream, and second, we fully intend to practise it in the spiritual integration of the races.

"Students do not run the schools, so we cannot make the decisions which will officially discard the Jim Crow system in Catholic education. But we do pray that at least in the colleges the integration of whites and Negroes will soon take place. We are preparing for that by learning to know each other while the schools are still separate. We are participating in interracial activities both on and off the campus. We are more ready for this religious, educational, and democratic unity than some college administrators think. Any white student who will resign from college when Negro Catholics are admitted does not understand what it means to be a practising Catholic.

"What are we waiting for? More and more Negroes are getting a college education. They are questioning the whole illogical system of segregation. Young Negroes are directing their questions to the Church, to the white Catholics, to the young Catholics, to the Southern Catholics. We white Southern Catholic college students are willing to give them a straight answer; we shall not cease our labors until the split in the Mystical Body is joined together again through the love of Christ.

"The die-hards are fearful people and often deeply prejudiced. Where would the Church of Christ be today if the Apostles had been guided by the same kind of do-nothing attitude? We thank God that the spirit of the Apostles is not dead today, and that in some small way we Catholic college students can promote their mission of universal love."*

THE CATHOLIC INTERRACIAL COUNCIL

With the formation of the Catholic Interracial Council of New York City on Pentecost Sunday, 1934, a group of distinguished Catholic laymen of both races, white and colored, collected the experiences of these various movements and projects and launched for the first time a specific and carefully organized program for interracial justice. Much of the program's formulation was the outcome of six years of previous prayer, meditation, and discussion among a zealous group of Catholic professional and businessmen, largely Negro, in the New York metropolitan area known as the Catholic Laymen's Union. In co-operation with the Clergy Conference on Negro Welfare, the Catholic Interracial Council established a Catholic Interracial Center at 20 Vesey Street, New York City—also the publication office of the Council's monthly, *Interracial Review*—a center of information, public discussion, and assistance to the twenty-eight other Catholic interracial councils which since that time have been set up in various urban centers of the country, under the auspices of the respective Catholic bishops.

---

* "The South is making headway in working out the answer to its race problems. Progress is slower than Christian charity and justice demand and slower than progressive democracy demands, but the answer is coming—and sooner than most of us think.

"The old-line politicians are far behind the rest of the South in their attitude on racial problems. They are fighting hard for the status quo but it is a rear guard action" (Rev. Louis J. Twomey, S.J., Loyola University, New Orleans).

THREE GUIDEPOSTS

Three basic considerations guided the new approach to the problem of race relations, as seen from the Catholic viewpoint (the Catholic interracial movement):

(1) The Church's ministry, spiritual and cultural, to the people of a racial minority is bound to be frustrated and to defeat its own end of gaining souls and forming good Christians—an honor to Church and country—unless it vindicates the entire, integral dignity of those to whom it ministers. It is concerned not with Negroes alone, or with any other race or people alone, but simply with human beings who share the needs and problems common to all mankind.

(2) In a matter where human rights are concerned, where misconceptions are so gross, deep-rooted, plausible and prevalent, no effective progress can be made without creating a new *climate of opinion.* The apostle of interracial justice among highly prejudiced fellow citizens resembles in many ways the missionary conversing with a foreign people bound by ancient tribal customs and taboos. Direct assault will not dislodge the fetishes. The idols will bow out only when people have become sufficiently enlightened to wish to remove them of themselves. Hence, basic to the situation is a program of education, in the sense of public relations for the truth: in the words of Archbishop Roberts, to "commend to people" the authority of the Christian law of love and justice. "By reason of your profession," said Pope Pius XII to the Negro publishers in May, 1946, "you are favorably circumstanced to influence thousands of readers, and no doubt you make it a primary purpose of your writing to counsel them aright in their pursuit of that interracial justice and brotherhood which alone can secure the stability of all that

71

men prize . . . fraternal charity should be welded ever more firmly through the efforts of all men of good will. With this prayer in Our heart, and with deep, fatherly affection We invoke on you and on all who labor with you in charity to further the cause of interracial justice, the blessing of almighty God."

The spiritual citadels to be captured are not the bishops and chanceries of the Church. These have long since declared their official position. It is the mass of the Catholic people, on the religious side; just as on the civic side the basic task is the education of the community at large.

This stress on an educational program is not to be understood in a defeatist sense, as if, when abuses are evident, no representations were to be made to properly constituted authorities. When such abuses occur, recourse is necessary, just as in the civic sphere all the educational programs in the world will not dispense us from the obligation of taking recourse to courts, judges and legislators when such appeal is needed and opportune. It is rather a question of primary emphasis: marshaling the many obvious and legitimate means for influencing the public mind; means that are used for any good and worthy cause, such as methodical presentation through the various channels of communication: platform, pulpit, radio, television, the press, news services, public forums, private conferences, books, pamphlets, lectures, etc. It would include a dignified and effective representation in the policy-making circles of national organizations. It means considering this question as a man-sized problem in public relations, to be handled in a man-sized way: on a local and more intimate scale; on a bold and national level; and, where pertinent, even on a world scale.

(3) Last, but not least, a lesson indicated by the disappointed experience of the Federated Colored Catholics applies in this instance. The disadvantages that afflict the members of a given racial group cannot be treated merely as the concern

of the disadvantaged group alone: they can only be treated adequately and successfully by the *joint action of all concerned*. This means, in this particular instance, that members of both races should work for a common interest. Although the Negro is the victim of discrimination, he does not necessarily know the answer or the cure. This is another reason why the Catholic interracial movement should include both races working together. The Negro, in short, can hardly achieve full recognition in society by his own unaided exertions, however dramatic and heroic. The white man cannot in justice refuse to act until the Negro fulfils certain arbitrarily fixed requirements. On the other hand, the Negro cannot afford to postpone his own action until the day when the white man has finally seen the light. Work for interracial justice is of its own nature interracial. It bespeaks the co-operation of both races, not in a merely formal, "token" fashion, but as a genuine and sincere co-operation, based upon real friendship and personal, day-by-day collaboration. It means, furthermore, the co-operation of the laity with their clergy and their bishops along with thoroughly generous lay initiative, and the co-operation of Catholics with men of good will outside the Church.

NEGRO LEADERSHIP

"It is a national reproach that the Negro leader must continue even in a time of crisis to divert his energies to problems that would never arise but for the existence of denials and discriminations. The blame may be attributed to the attitudes of prejudice or indifference that characterize a great portion of the white population. With so much to be done for his own group the Negro must continually neglect from the community and its problems in an effort to persuade white Americans to recognize and practise the principles of interracial justice implicit in the Bill of Rights. If basic rights are to be achieved for the race it is imperative that the Negro leader must make this the primary goal even at the risk of being called an absentee leader rather than a vital, down-to-earth promoter of Negro community enterprise.

"Fully as urgent and important as Negro leadership is the leadership among white groups, among students, professional men, businessmen and workers in industry, devoted to creating an interracial basis for a more truly equitable and humane order.

"There is an immensely vast potential cultural and economic wealth in the millions of America's Negro people. Some of it has been developed, to the mutual enrichment of Negro and white, but what still lies untouched, what is still to be released, is beyond our capacity to estimate."[*]

In the words of U.S. Assistant Secretary of Labor J. Ernest Wilkins, at the Founders Day observance at Dillard University, New Orleans, on October 31, 1954:

"Ultimately, all of the slogans and all of our good intentions crumble into the dust of our vanity unless our lives are dedicated to serving God. It is not the role of Negroes in America to achieve interracial justice, but to achieve justice. It is not the role of Negroes in America to achieve only racial integration, but to achieve the association of free men dedicated to justice. It is within our power to give strength and fiber to the convictions which America professes, and to give witness to the faith from which our freedom springs."

[*] Thomas F. Doyle, "The Plight of Negro Leadership," *Interracial Review,* February, 1942, pp. 23–25.

PART III

The Catholic Position: Principles

In discussing the Church's position on the racial question, certain fundamental truths should be kept in mind:

(1) All men, since they have been created by the same God, are sons of the same eternal Father and hence enjoy the same fundamental human dignity and rights.

(2) Jesus Christ lived, died, and rose from the dead in order to redeem all men and confer upon them the same supernatural dignity and rights as members of His Mystical Body.

The Church holds that fundamental human rights are not something conferred by the State or by any other human institution. They are not the result of mere social conventions or current folkways. Basic human rights, as such, are equal in all human beings, even though in *other* matters—personal merit, culture, native or acquired ability—people are usually unequal. This equality of rights derives from the essential dignity and destiny of the human being as such, a being created by an all-wise and infinitely loving God in order to enjoy, by his own deliberate choice, eternal happiness in union with his Creator and origin. Hence, in the Christian concept, man's essential dignity does not arise from anything apart from his relationship to his Creator and last end. Man does not create his own sublime worth out of his own littleness, but enjoys it by his very nature as a creature of God and—through the gift of divine grace —an heir of heaven. In the words of the German religious philosopher, Romano Guardini: *"In der Achtung, mit der Du, O Gott, mich achtest, ist meine Würde begründet. In deiner Ehre ruht meine Ehre."* (My own dignity is based, O God, upon the respect that You bear for my own being. My honor rests in Your honor.)

The Church is likewise deeply solicitous for those whose spiritual, social, or cultural position has been retarded because they have been deprived of the exercise of human rights. Pope Pius XII expressed this solicitude in his letter to the American hierarchy: "We confess that we feel a special paternal affection, which is certainly inspired by heaven, for the Negro people dwelling among you; for in the field of religion and education we know they need special care and comfort and are very deserving of it . . . We pray fruitful success for those whose generous zeal is devoted to their welfare."[*]

Hence, the Catholic Church does not look upon the race problem as a mere problem of social adjustment: how can we best figure out from experience ways and means for people to get along together? As Chester Bowles says: "It is not a question primarily to be solved by laws and law courts, even though these are both useful and necessary in guaranteeing our rights. It is essentially a *moral* problem,"[†] a question of right and wrong, of sin and justice. Since the Catholic Church believes that men can and do sin against their Creator, and can be held accountable for their sins, she will not excuse violations of basic rights as mere matters of unkindness or lack of delicacy. Race

[*] *Sertum Laetitiae,* Nov. 1, 1939, as translated in *Catholic Mind,* Vol. 37, p. 923.
[†] "The Negro, Progress and Challenge," *New York Times Magazine,* February 7, 1954.

prejudice, discrimination, and compulsory racial segregation are morally sinful.

There are two approaches to Catholic teaching on racial problems: one of reason and one of faith. Reason and faith are not opposed; they complement one another. The Church respects reason and the scientific research developed by reasoning. Our natural reasoning powers are impaired, but they are not destroyed, as a consequence of the sin of our first parents. Weakened as they are by passion and greed, particularly in matters of human relations, those powers can be strengthened and rehabilitated by the grace of God. Jesus Christ, our supreme Teacher and Founder of our faith, frequently calls on ordinary human reason and good sense, in order to enforce His sublime lessons. Although His basic appeal is to the lofty motives of supernatural love, He nevertheless asks us to study and weigh the considerations that stem from ordinary human experience.

A cold, purely intellectual approach to the problems of living, suffering, and aspiring human beings is doomed to ultimate sterility. Simon-pure social science or simon-pure political science is not the effective answer. Nevertheless, genuine science —documented knowledge, armed with the techniques of modern methodology—is not only a powerful but an indispensable aid in the service of the higher charity. The divinely inspired Good Samaritan used very practical means in dealing with the wounded victim on the road to Jericho.

THE SCIENTIFIC APPROACH

The genuinely Catholic viewpoint on race relations takes into account the body of sound, reasoned knowledge which intelligent study of this question has accumulated, particularly in the United States, over a period of nearly one hundred years. Some of the main points of this doctrine we can sum up as follows:

(1) Precisely because the racial question deeply affects our sentiments and instincts, we cannot successfully deal with it in the heat of emotion and passion. Wherever any particular issue is at stake, our first approach will be to assemble the facts. In the words of Marshal Foch, France's leader in World War I, we shall first ask: "What is it all about?" We will make a special study of the many ways by which clear reasoning can be side-tracked by various deceptive devices, such as hasty generalizations and stereotypes. Catholics, as do Protestants and Jews, deeply resent the use of these mental and rhetorical structures when applied to their own religious affiliation. Our insight into the falsity and injustice of such constructs when applied to the field of religion or nationality should alert us to their deceptiveness in the case of people of differing races.

(2) A rational approach to the race problem will expose the error of racialism: the myth of inherently superior or inferior races. Science and religion unite in condemning this error. In the words of Francis Cardinal Spellman, Archbishop of New York, who sent congratulations on September 27, 1949, for an anniversary celebration, to the National Association for the Advancement of Colored People:

"The Church repudiates, as abhorrent to her very nature, the pernicious doctrine that men are born with the stamp upon them of essential racial superiority or inferiority. She recognizes no master race, but proclaims the God-given equality before God of all souls, for whose salvation our blessed Redeemer suffered and sacrificed. In making this assertion I am but stating Catholic doctrine and re-echoing the teachings of our present revered Pontiff, Pope Pius XII, who at the beginning of his term of office declared that the spirit and the teachings of the Church can never be other than that which the Apostle of the Gentiles preached: 'That in the Church there is neither Gentile or Jew, circumcision or uncircumcision, barbarian or Scythian, slave or free. But Christ is all in all.' "

Quite apart from religious considerations, science itself also repudiates as absurd and harmful to society the idea that any group of people, by the very nature of their psycho-physical makeup is essentially superior to any other human group. Or, to express the same idea in other words, science rejects the notion of inherited racial inferiority.*

The late Rev. John M. Cooper, professor of anthropology at The Catholic University of America, frequently exposed this fallacy in his lectures and writings. In Dr. Cooper's words:

"The assumption by many whites that the white race in general and the Nordic in particular is superior to the Negro race is based in the main on two supposed lines of evidence, that of intelligence tests and that of cultural achievement.

"As for the tests, in the majority of tests made, the whites have scored higher than the Negroes. This would look like strong presumptive evidence were it not for two important considerations that are sometimes overlooked. First, in a minority at least of such comparative tests, the Negro has scored higher than the whites. Second, into these gross scores have entered many factors, such as differences in social status, in cultural background, in education, in language ability, in racial mixture and in degree of interest in or emotional reaction to the tests themselves. Until the role these variable factors play and have played in comparative tests of Negro and white intelligence has been accurately measured and allowed for, it is not pos-

* "Race is an emotional concept, not a scientific one. Skin color is of minor importance in physical anthropology. If we accept the evolutionary theory that the farther man progresses from the anthropoid, the more advanced he is, we find the negroid most advanced and the white nearer the anthropoid. Every race, however has its share of geniuses and morons, and anthropology contends that it is people, not race, that count" (Rev. J. Franklin Ewing, S.J., of Fordham University).

81

sible to draw any scientific conclusion as to comparative mentality of the Negro on the one hand and on the other of the white race in general or of the Nordic in particular.

"Finally, what of cultural achievement? In reality the Nordics, so far as we can discover scientifically, contributed very little indeed to the progress of human culture up to within four or five centuries ago. If actual cultural achievement were a scientific index to racial intelligence, the Nordic would, at least up to about 1500, have been in about the same box with the Negro, on about the same level of racial intelligence. In fact, there would have been fairly good ground for concluding that the Negro represented a somewhat higher mentality than the Nordic, for, all things considered, the Negro in Africa probably had greater cultural achievements to his credit than had the Nordic up to the beginning of the modern period that dawned with the era of the great geographical discoveries."*

THE CHURCH CONDEMNS RACISM

As Cardinal Spellman says, there can be no doubt about Catholic teaching in this matter. In the last few decades, the exaltation of pride of race by nazis and fascists, and their contempt and scorn for "inferior races," drew stern rebuke from both Pius XI and our present Holy Father, Pius XII.

In his encyclical *Mit Brennender Sorge*, on the condition of the Church in Germany, issued on March 14, 1937, Pius XI declared: "As God's sun shines on all that bear human countenance, so does His law know no privileges or exceptions. . . . Only superficial minds can lapse into the heresy of speaking of a national God, or a national religion; only such can make the

* "Negro and Nordic," *Interracial Review*, May, 1934, pp. 58–59.

mad attempt of trying to confine within the boundaries of a single people, within the narrow blood stream of a single race, God, the Creator of the world."

And Pius XII in his first encyclical, *Summi Pontificatus*, issued on October 20, 1939, spoke of "a marvelous vision which makes us see the human race in the unity of one common origin in God, 'one God and Father of all, who is above all and in us all' (Ephesians 4:6); in the unity of human nature, which in every man is equally composed of material body and spiritual, immortal soul; in the unity of the immediate end and mission in the world; in the unity of dwelling place, the earth, of whose resources all men by natural right avail themselves to sustain life and develop life; in the unity of the supernatural end, God Himself, to whom all should tend in the unity of means to secure that end."

These principles are widely recognized today, even though many do not follow them in practice. Very few in this country today, and practically no one in any position of responsibility, would be willing to make public profession of a doctrine of racial superiority or of "white supremacy."

Even the politicians who have most strongly opposed the Supreme Court's decision outlawing segregation in schools have been careful to avoid any imputation that Negroes are "inferior." And the espousals of such a doctrine by Calvinist theologians in the Union of South Africa who support the dominant National Party's racial policies have evoked widespread condemnation in non-Catholic as well as Catholic circles.

Against the background of recent events in Mississippi and elsewhere, the National Council of Churches of Christ (Protestant) declared on October 5, 1955: "The National Council of Churches defends the rights and liberties of cultural, racial and religious minorities. The insecurity of one menaces the security of all. Christians must be especially sensitive to the oppression of minorities."

THE COST OF INEQUALITY

(3) Scientific reason, however, is not content with merely exploding the "myth of race." It has accumulated a wealth of data explaining many of those human appearances which seem to lend a handle to the race theory, and that cannot be left out of consideration. Social psychology reveals many of the real causes of inequality between various racial or social groups. It shows how such inequality is the result, not of fancied racial defects, but of human factors, which normally would produce the same effects in any other people subjected to the same influences over a sufficient length of time. Poor schools and poor teaching produce backward citizens. Lack of incentive discourages any sense of vigorous social or political responsibility. People incur collective neuroses as the result of being relentlessly identified with a former subject race. An intelligent study of publicly accessible statistics will—or should—convince anyone of the heavy price we pay, as a nation, for indulging in racial prejudice.

The sheer cost to the public, for instance, of our slum areas, which are perpetuated through the pressure of racial prejudice and racial discrimination, needs to be taken into account. It is estimated as high as a billion dollars a year for the nation. The researchers of the National Urban League, in a recent study, ascertained that the slum areas of a city pay, on the average 6 per cent of a city's taxes. But they account for 45 per cent of a city's police cost, 35 per cent of its fire cost, contribute 55 per cent of its delinquency. Somebody has to pay. The slums do not.

The taxpayer *does*. For public services he pays a sum far out of proportion to what he gets out of them himself.

Characteristic of the slum is the *rent squeeze*. In a big city, rents are usually high, as the result of crowding. To have the advantages of living in a big city, people will pay higher rents. However, when people can move freely in a big city and live where they like, rents—like water—will find a level. When people are hemmed in, as Negroes often are by discrimination, rents rise, like water behind a dam. Negroes pay rents disproportionate to the type of building they inhabit. To pay rents that barely maintain old buildings, rather than build or support new ones, New York City's Negro families are forced to divert approximately $200,000,000 from other more productive expenditures.

Proportionate, also, to the losses which slum areas inflict upon the nation would be the amount that Negroes—or other victims of job discrimination—could add to the local or the national income if they were free to seek and fill jobs commensurate with their abilities. It has been estimated, says President Eisenhower's Committee on Government contracts, that the nation's sixteen million Negroes now have an annual personal income exceeding $15,000,000,000. If equal employment opportunity were universal, billions of dollars in additional purchasing power would be created. Communities are forced to expend large sums of tax money to counteract delinquency, crime, and other social maladjustments which can be traced to discrimination in employment. Everybody pays this bill. Non-discriminatory employment reduces this bill. Companies that give employment on a basis of qualifications alone are able to hire the person with the best training and experience available for the job. They increase their labor supply. All workers gain from equal job opportunities, not only those who have been subjected to discrimination. Unions strengthen their economic position under uniform standards of pay, hiring, upgrading, promotion and lay-off for workers. A divided work force is a weak work force. Equal job opportunity improves our relations and strengthens our position among nations. Discrimination weakens the moral position of the United States in the world, gives communists an opportunity to play up racial bigotry and creates anti-American sentiment.

Where business has followed an enlightened racial program, it has contributed to the social and economic welfare of the community and the country. In this way, business has built good will for itself and increased its potential consumer market. Considerations of this kind have led to laws directed against unfair employment practices and created the New York State Commission against Discrimination. They also lie behind the work of agencies like the National Urban League, and its branches in fifty-five cities of the United States. Much has been won, but there is still a long distance to go.

PREJUDICE NOT NECESSARY

In the matter of race prejudice itself, a patient and impartial study of the data at hand has led to an ever-wider acceptance among American citizens of a number of elementary conclusions very different from those jumped at by those who judge merely from appearances and hearsay. Many people have never taken the trouble to test current wisecracks and slogans by careful examination. Some of the most important of these conclusions are the following.

(1) Race prejudice is not a necessary, inborn attribute. Children, for instance, are usually not prejudiced, until they have learned racial attitudes from their parents or from other older members of the community. When parents impose pressures

upon their children in order that the child shall have a higher
esteem for respectability and conformity—in other words,
when Mother or Father tell little Johnny or Susan that you just
don't talk in too friendly a way to any Negroes or Negro children because it's something that "our kind of people" don't do—
they are fostering the roots of racial prejudice in the child.
When people say: "I know I oughtn't to be prejudiced, but I
am just born that way and can't help it," they are uttering a
falsehood. Certainly, most of us find it difficult, often impossible, to change our natural likes and dislikes. Early impressions
and a multitude of associations fix those emotional reactions in
our minds. But, though our feelings are largely beyond our control, we can learn not to let our feelings sway our judgments,
and we can be held responsible if we base our deliberate actions upon mere sentiments and not upon our reasoned knowledge of the true facts concerning our neighbor.

(2) Prejudice, accordingly, can be cured, for we learn to act
from better knowledge, and to acquire that knowledge through
the many channels open to us. How many people, for instance, have never actually listened to a foreigner, a person
of another nationality or culture, or a Negro or Oriental, explain *his* or *her* case in his own way. Yet, after they have had
that experience, people testify to the complete change of attitude that it produced. Perhaps the reader can ask himself: how
many times in my life have I heard an intelligent American
Indian, for instance, explain why the Indians feel as strongly as
they do about certain types of American legislation. Have I
listened to a Negro student or businessman, or a Negro nun, tell
of their interests and their efforts to develop the talents that
God has given them? From such personal testimony we can
learn how individuals and whole populations are able to emerge
from the depressed conditions that are the result of prejudice,

and fit themselves to take a worthy part in the community of citizens as a whole.

Knowledge of facts, too, will prevent the contrary evil: that of exaggerated sensitivity in the matter of racial prejudice: imagining it where it does not exist; seeing insults where none are intended—the chip-on-the-shoulder attitude.

(3) Where racial segregation is enforced upon people, either in a residential neighborhood or, for instance, in a public housing project, the net effect is not such as to lessen group prejudice, but rather to increase it. People who never see each other at all, and have no contact whatsoever, are simply indifferent, and have neither prejudice nor non-prejudice. There is, as far as I know, no sentiment against the Eskimo among the Zulus, nor do the North Africans bear hard feelings against the Finns. But when different groups live more or less side by side in the same local or national community and know of each other's existence, hear continually stories about each other, and sense a continual group rivalry, then a rigid separation is a seed ground for a growing suspicion and dislike. Some of the most bitter and unreasoning divisions I have seen among Catholic people of different races have come, as I have personally witnessed, after the conflicting parish elements had been separated and consigned to separate places of worship. Some well-meaning but misguided individual had judged that in that way he could ensure peace between supposedly conflicting elements.

PUBLIC HOUSING PATTERNS

In the field of public housing this question readily comes into play. We can either house people according to their needs, without regard to their race, religion, or national origin, or we can create, as we have done in the past, segregated communities.

The common pattern in public housing outside the New York metropolitan district is complete segregation, with Negroes and whites living in separate housing projects, but there are important exceptions.*

Careful comparison between the racial attitudes resulting from either of these types of housing appears to indicate that when people of like qualifications, like fitness for neighborly relations, live in proximity to one another there is a corresponding growth of desire for friendly relations. On the other hand, where people live separately there is less concern about achieving social peace.

Human behavior tends to be rationalized and tends to set up patterns conformable to such rationalizing, patterns in law and in public policy. If we are convinced that we cannot on any account live near to a person of another race, and adopt that as a principle, we naturally think up reasons and excuses for justifying our conduct. If I *cannot* permit myself or anyone else to live in the building with Negro tenants, I shall come to think that there must be something intrinsically harmful about them as Negroes.

In no other field has prejudice remained so virulent and common as in that of housing. It seems to be the only remaining interracial problem producing fairly regular violence. As barriers to equality are overcome in employment, public accommodations and education, the housing field becomes conspicuous by virtue of its widespread, rigid, and persistent discriminatory patterns.†

* Deutsch and Collins, *Interracial Housing* (University of Minnesota Press, 1950).
† "Housing is the key to the employment situation in the new industrial centers. Experience with anti-Negro discrimination in housing has

When we seek the reasons for this condition, we find that discriminatory barriers in housing seem to be almost the *sine qua non* of prejudice. Men reflect their *true* values, ideas, and attitudes most directly in the intimate primary realm of living that surrounds the home. Discriminatory barriers in housing are strong because they are probably the last citadel for those basic attitudes of racial antipathy which, we must admit, still exist in the minds of the majority of white people. The idea of integration in housing directly challenges this citadel and the attitudes it represents. Integration in housing, therefore, has much deeper implication than integration in any other area of social intercourse. Acceptance of the Negro as an equal in employment, education, or community facilities is a good sign, but these areas are relatively impersonal. It is commonly observed how people can participate in impersonal situations where racial justice prevails, yet in other situations still hold the most unjust racial attitudes. It is almost impossible, however, to conceive of practising racial justice in the intimate institutions of home and neighborhood and at the same time harboring unjust racial attitudes.

All of these reasons explain why there is a certain finality about integration in housing in relation to the whole race relations problem. Many believe that when integration in housing is common, the race-relations problem will have been dealt its

proven that it is possible to exclude any group from employment by excluding it from housing. No skilled worker wants to subject his family to discriminatory policies in housing or in any other area of community life.

"These problems represent a challenge to develop leaders in human and race relations if we are to avoid building communities with 1952 steel mills and 1852 race relations. Capable leaders can educate long-time residents of expanding areas to look upon the new groups as potential assets to the community and keep open to them the doors of their community centers, churches and other community facilities" (R. Maurice Moss, Associate Executive Director of the National Urban League).

death blow. From this point of view, housing has always been the central issue in race relations, the final acid test which race relations progress must meet.*

The effective answer to false reasoning is first and foremost to destroy the false pattern that has mothered it.

THE APPROACH OF FAITH

Our Christian faith confirms the findings of natural morality. Jesus Himself, the Author of our faith, declared expressly that He did not come in order to abolish a jot or tittle of God's law, and severely rebuked those who violated it. The fundamental rights of all men can be grouped under four headings: the right to physical, moral, intellectual and social integrity. By the *right to physical integrity* is meant the right to a full physical life; hence, the right not to be unfairly impeded in the legitimate search for food, clothing, shelter, marriage, a home, decent working conditions, wages, medical and hospital care, and recreation.

By the *right to moral integrity* we mean the right to know God and His holy will, and all that such knowledge implies; hence, the right to religious and moral education, the right to worship God and receive the sacraments and share with others in the opportunities for advancing in the spiritual life.

By the *right to intellectual integrity* is meant the right to intellectual training in accord with one's capacities and the concrete opportunities offered, whether by State or Church institutions.

By the *right to social integrity* is meant the right to live in peace as a fully accepted and respected member of the com-

* John McDermott and Dennis Clark, "Helping the Panic Neighborhood," *Interracial Review*, August, 1955.

munity, to associate in harmony with one's neighbors, to make friends with those who find friendship acceptable, and to give and receive from all, without hindrance or humiliation, the common signs of courtesy which human dignity demands.

Enumerating these same rights, Pope Pius XII, in his 1942 Christmas allocution, declared: "He who would have the star of peace shine out and stand over society should co-operate, for his part, in giving back to the human person the dignity given it by God from the beginning."*

In the light of the above principles, supported as they are by authoritative Catholic teaching, there can be no doubt that the fundamental rights of the Negro or any other citizen in this country are all too often violated by the practice of race segregation, whether it apply to schools and institutions of higher learning, hospitals and other institutions, public transportation, and public accommodation. To that extent, at least, such practices are violations of natural justice and thus seriously sinful. The same would apply to the refusal of employment to qualified workers on racial grounds. As far as a person's rights are concerned, it makes little difference whether this refusal comes directly from the employer or indirectly, through exclusion from the labor unions. These principles apply to violation of basic human rights through legislation or intimidation preventing the vote and the exercise of his other political or civic rights. They apply when a citizen is unable to obtain protection from violence, or when he is subjected to segregatory practices. Many of these aim to limit his natural right to choose his own place of residence on an equal footing with all other citizens, regardless of race, color, or creed.

In a pastoral letter read at all Masses on Sunday, February 19, 1956, Most Rev. Joseph Francis Rummel, Archbishop of

* As translated in *Catholic Mind*, Vol. 41, January, 1943, pp. 49–50.

New Orleans, condemned racial segregation as morally sinful on three counts:

"(1) Racial segregation as such is morally wrong and sinful because it is a denial of the unity and solidarity of the human race as conceived by God in the creation of man in Adam and Eve. . . .

"(2) Racial segregation is morally wrong and sinful because it is a denial of the unity and universality of the Redemption. The eternal Son of God, Christ Jesus our Lord, came into the world to redeem and save all men, to die for all men on the cross, to make the life of grace available through the Church and the sacraments for all men, to embrace all men in His Mystical Body on earth and in the life of glory in Heaven. Racial segregation would draw the color line across the inspiring plan of the Redemption and thus sin against the divine providence, the love and the mercy that conceived and carried out the wonderful mystery. . . .

"(3) Racial segregation is morally wrong and sinful because it is basically a violation of the dictates of justice and the mandate of love, which in obedience to God's will must regulate the relations between all men. To deny to members of a certain race, just because they are members of that race, certain rights and opportunities, civic or economic, educational or religious, recreational or social, imposes upon them definite hardships and humiliations, frustrations and impediments to progress which condemn them to perpetual degradation which is only a step removed from slavery. Such indignities are grievous violations of Christian justice and charity, which cannot be justified in this modern age of enlightenment and loudly proclaimed democracy."

NATURAL RIGHTS

The official teachings of the Church in recent times strongly emphasize the principles of natural justice. The Popes in their encyclicals, the archbishops and bishops of the United States, constantly recur to our duties in this respect. Pope Leo XIII in his encyclical "On the Condition of the Workingman" (*Rerum Novarum*), Pope Pius XI in his encyclicals "On the Reconstruction of the Social Order" (*Quadragesimo Anno*) and "On Atheistic Communism" (*Divini Redemptoris*), as well as our present Pontiff, Pope Pius XII, declare the right of all human beings, as human beings, with all the responsibility that this entails—to own some private property, to receive adequate and fair wages for work honestly done, on behalf of themselves and their families; to organize for this end, to enjoy decent habitations and decent living conditions in general.

It is easy to preach thrift, but thrift, as was pointed out by Pope Pius XI in *Quadragesimo Anno* (1931), depends on certain conditions in order to operate. "If a workman's wages be sufficient to enable him comfortably to support himself, his wife, and his children, he will find it easy, if he be a sensible man, to practise thrift; and he will not fail, by cutting down expenses to put by some little savings and thus secure a modest source of income. Nature itself would urge him to do this."

Certainly, the hope of private property, the possibility of private property, is one of the most indispensable conditions of thrift, and if this applies to all citizens it applies with particular force to the Negro, for whom private property was in former years completely banned. And so the Pope continues: "We have seen that this great labor question cannot be solved save by assuming as a principle that private ownership must be held

sacred and inviolable. The law, therefore, should favor ownership, and its policy should be to induce as many as possible of
the people to become owners."

Many a bitter prejudice has to be overcome to achieve such
obvious and simple results. But again the Pope speaks with encouragement: "Prejudice, it is true, is mighty, and so is the
greed of money; but if the sense of what is just and rightful be
not deliberately stifled, their fellow citizens are sure to be won
over by a kindly feeling toward men whom they see to be in
earnest as regards their work and who prefer unmistakably
right dealing to mere lucre and the sacredness of duty to every
other consideration." It is clear to any observant person that the
Negro community illustrates in practically every detail the lessons taught by *Quadragesimo Anno*.

The key to many basic elements of the Negro problem lies
in the social insight of three great social-minded popes: Leo
XIII, Pius XI, and Pius XII. This does not mean that the Negro
question is treated as such. But the problems of classes, workers, and intellectuals alike are treated. The procedure is direct.
First, we recognize that the Negro is a human being who pos-
sesses a human soul. Then, we know that the range of the development of the human soul is infinite. Finally, we can find
the correct appraisal of the American Negro in terms of human
freedom, Christian spirit and an earnestness to correct man-
made abuses of human liberty and welfare. Questions of the
rights of workers, the place of classes in their right categories,
and, finally, the realization that the American Negro comprises
all classes, and that he is denied the right to participate in all
privileges: these can be seen more clearly in the light of
Quadragesimo Anno. Only the fear of burdening these pages
by too many quotations keeps me from constantly referring to
the 1942 Christmas allocution of Pope Pius XII, which treats so
lucidly of the scheme of mutual rights and duties.

FUNCTION OF AUTHORITY

The Church likewise teaches the duty, according to natural law, of public authority—the State or government—to guarantee these rights and enforce the corresponding duties.* Authority's role was noted by Very Rev. Laurence J. McGinley, S.J., President of Fordham University, in his sermon to the Catholic Lawyers Guild on October 2, 1955:

"A Negro child, born to the image of God in Mississippi, has a potential freedom, a free will, a power of choosing good or evil. But the freedom for which his father died in far Korea is not this innate power—nor is it the opportunity for his child to embrace what is good or evil. It is rather the opportunity for his child and for all men to achieve a mature freedom, an adult and virtuous autonomy, consistently choosing the true and good because the law of virtue rules through reason. The opportunity for this adult freedom, this anticipation of virtue, exists only in a balanced society. It is authority's task to provide and protect it."

Where the sacred rights of the human personality and the integrity of Christian education are concerned, a truly preventive care, inspired by Christian charity and love of souls, can co-operate with legitimate authority. In such a case, it is our duty and our high privilege as Catholics to respect such legitimate authority, both as to letter and as to spirit.

When Jesuit High School of Dallas, Texas, accepted two Negro applicants for the fall semester, 1955, it was the first time

---

* "From the juridic order, as willed by God, flows man's inalienable right to juridic society, and by this very fact to a definite sphere of rights, immune from all arbitrary attack" (Pius XII, Christmas allocution, 1942, as translated in *Catholic Mind*, Vol. 41, p. 57).

Negro students had been admitted to an all-white Dallas high school. In explaining the school's position, Rev. Thomas Shields, S.J., the President, and Rev. Michael P. Kammer, S.J., the Principal, issued the following joint statement:

"Jesuit High School understands that integration is a vexing problem for many people. On the other hand, it is our conviction that all citizens of this country should obey the Constitution and the laws as they are interpreted by the Supreme Court.

"The will of the Court in this case is clear. While the decree does not extend to private institutions, its spirit plainly does.

"Jesuit High School, although not a public but a private educational institution of the Catholic Church, is thoroughly American and is committed to adherence to the Government of the United States and its Supreme Court."

AUTHORITY AND LEADERSHIP

The decision taken by the authorities of Jesuit High School in Dallas respects the unanimous, prompt attitude shown by the Catholic archbishop and bishops in fourteen states shortly before and immediately after the Supreme Court's historic decree.

A survey was made by the National Catholic Welfare Conference shortly after the May 17, 1954, Supreme Court decision. In the fourteen states where the schools were segregated either by law or by custom, the survey found that Catholic schools were definitely straightening the path toward racial integration. In many instances where the public schools were just beginning to move toward desegregation, or were still delaying action, the parochial schools had been successfully integrated for several years. In some areas of the deep South the pressure of long-standing social custom cautioned those responsible for Catholic education to withhold action until the Supreme Court had outlined its program and public opinion had become more used to the idea. But even in the "wait-and-see" dioceses, the general pattern was for the Church to press for calm and quick acceptance of the fact that school segregation is now unconstitutional. In some, it was understood, race barriers were actually being swept away, but without public announcement.

The Supreme Court decision is legally binding only on the public schools. The general reaction of the Church has been that the will of the Court imposes a moral obligation on Catholic schools, since, as Fathers Shields and Kammer say, the will of the Court is clear. It opens the way legally for the Church to make her benefits equally available to all races.

In point of fact, Catholic schools in various parts of the South had already started integration before the Supreme Court decree.

The decree brought no novelty to the Catholic school pupils in the nation's capital. Under the leadership of Archbishop Patrick A. O'Boyle of Washington, the parochial and archdiocesan schools of the capital and its Maryland suburbs had been enrolling youngsters without regard to race since 1949.

The Catholic schools of St. Louis were completely integrated in 1947 by Archbishop Joseph E. Ritter after mixed groups had been attending parochial grammar schools for years, and St. Louis University (Catholic) had also long since opened all its departments to all races without distinction. Catholic schools in the diocese of St. Joseph, Missouri, made a similar policy effective in 1948, and the Kansas City, Missouri, diocese rounded out integration in the whole state the following year.

In Virginia, colored students since September, 1954, had already been attending three previously "white" Catholic high schools in Richmond and one in Roanoke, as well as grammar schools in Roanoke, the tidewater area and the northern counties near Washington. Bishop Peter L. Ireton of Richmond had announced just prior to the Supreme Court ruling that Negroes would be welcome in the Richmond Catholic high schools. In North Carolina, the five Catholic diocesan and parochial high schools were instructed in May, 1954, by Bishop Vincent S. Waters of Raleigh to accept all Catholic high-school students "no matter to what race they belong." The letter also asked that Negro Catholics be admitted to the elementary schools and hospitals. Other similar instances where integration, either in whole or in part, became the school's policy were Belmont Abbey College, in North Carolina, and its sister institution, Sacred Heart Academy, a junior college for girls; the Catholic schools of Arkansas, under Bishop Albert L. Fletcher of Little Rock; of Oklahoma, at the direction of Bishop Eugene J. McGuinness of Oklahoma City and Tulsa. In Texas, in the San Antonio area, there had been mixed schools for several years. Archbishop Robert E. Lucey of San Antonio announced in April, 1954, that complete integration was mandatory at all educational levels. In other Texas dioceses there was at least partial integration.

Following the Supreme Court's anti-segregation decision, the Catholic Committee of the South reprinted a portion of the statement made by the Southern bishops at its 1953 meeting. "There is no denying that there are certain practices and behavior patterns in the South, as in other parts of the country, which are alien to Christian principles and ideals," the bishops said. "The eradication of these practices and patterns was, and is to be, the task that must be undertaken before it is too late . . .

"We sincerely hope that the day will come when the ideal of Christian brotherhood will displace from our Southern scene all traces of the blight of racism. Let us Catholics, true to our convictions, set the pattern."

Duties to our neighbor apply with particular force in matters that touch upon the integrity of the home and of the requirements for livelihood, such as the use of unjust economic pressure. Hitler skilfully used this type of coercion during the period of his domination of Germany and Austria, and it is, of course, all-powerful in the hands of communists in our own day when they are in control.

Recent events have spotlighted this point. In South Carolina, as in some other Southern states, economic pressure had been exerted against Negroes who subscribed to school petitions sponsored by units of the National Association for the Advancement of Colored People.

In Orangeburg, South Carolina, for instance, a number of Negroes who signed such petitions had been dismissed from their jobs or—in the case of share-croppers or tenant farmers— told that their services would not be needed after this crop season. (The Catholic pastor of a Negro congregation in that city was obliged to drive forty miles each day in order to purchase milk for the school children of his parish.)

The names of all petitioners in the Charleston area had been published in the local newspapers. The city's biggest daily had suggested in an editorial that white citizens "study carefully" the lists of names and ask the signers their real intent in signing the petitions.

The Catholic Bishop of Charleston, Most Rev. John J. Russell, issued a statement on September 30, 1955, published over his signature on the front page of the *Catholic Banner* edition of *Our Sunday Visitor,* official weekly of the diocese. The statement did not specifically mention the race question, but its meaning was apparent:

"It is morally wrong and sinful to deprive a man of his job, to boycott his business, to deprive him of his livelihood, of the means of providing for his wife and family, when he has done

no wrong, but simply because he has exercised his constitutional right of petition.

"No Catholic can conscientiously have part in such unjust
practices. Our divine Lord said: 'What you do to the least of
these, my brethren, you do unto Me.' He also said: 'Love thy
neighbor as thyself.'"

THE PRIESTLY DIGNITY

How clear and definite the Church's teaching is in this matter is seen in the vigorous way in which she safeguards the
dignity of her own sacred ministers. This was dramatically illustrated in the much publicized incident that took place on October 2, 1955, in the archdiocese of New Orleans. On that date a
Negro Catholic priest, Rev. Gerald Lewis, S.V.D., was sent to
the little mixed congregation mission church at Jesuit Bend,
Louisiana, to celebrate Sunday Mass. He had had several warn-
ings that there would be trouble if he attempted to do so. But
he went ahead because on other occasions the difficulties had
not actually developed.

This time, however, when he reached the church, he found a
police car parked in the driveway and two armed men in uniform in a small group in front of the building. Three parishioners stopped him in the churchyard, telling him a Negro could
not say Mass in a white parish. "With the police standing
there," Father Lewis related, "my first thought was that this
was the law laying down a command. I just didn't argue." Later
he learned that the spokesman was the brother of a very important political figure in the area.

There was no trouble in the next church where he celebrated
the Holy Sacrifice. The pastor of the area told the delegation
not to interfere again. Both priests said they had numerous ex-

pressions of "shame" from throughout the United States, including the second church where Father Lewis officiated.

Archbishop Rummel of New Orleans suspended service at the Jesuit Bend church and reduced the number of Masses at two other churches until "the members of these communities express their willingness to accept for service in these churches whatever priest or priests we find it possible to send them."

The archbishop said in his letter to the parishioners that "this incident was clearly a violation of the obligation of reverence and devotion which Catholics owe to every priest of God, regardless of race, color or nationality.

"Every Catholic priest who enjoys the approval of his ecclesiastical superiors must be acceptable to our Catholic people, because as a priest he enjoys all the high qualifications which Holy Mother Church associates with his sublime dignity. . . .

"Furthermore, it is the teaching of Holy Mother Church that every human being, regardless of race, color, or nationality, is created after the image and likeness of God. . . . Thus, every human being, regardless of race, color, or nationality, is entitled to individual respect and consideration."

Those responsible for the affair "committed an act of injustice, uncharitableness and irreverence. They also violated the laws of the Church, which definitely forbid . . . the interference with the exercise of ecclesiastical authority or functions."

Osservatore Romano, Vatican City daily, published a vigorous front-page editorial calling Archbishop Rummel's action "prompt and admirable." The daily declared that racial exclusiveness is the "negation" of Roman Catholicism. "To use it against a priest by impeding him in the celebration of the Mass in which he pronounces the words of consecration intended by Christ for all believers in all times, in all countries, for all races, to forbid him to repeat the sacrifice is sacrilege," *Osservatore* said.

ADEQUATE LOVE

The Church does not teach these natural rights in an abstract, merely theoretical fashion. Nor does she appeal to mere sentiment. She adds a new and lofty motive over and above the call of sheer duty for the practice of natural justice: the motive of unselfish, Christlike love. Because as a Christian, as a Catholic, I genuinely love my fellow man, I desire that this love be the real article, not a hypocritical display. The Saviour rebuked those sons who professed filial piety but really violated their parents' natural rights by diverting to the Temple treasury (from which they got a kickback) the support to which their parents could rightfully lay claim.

If my love is genuine it will not fall short of its goal, it will be practical and adequate. The Samaritan whom Jesus praised in the Gospel was not satisfied with saying a kind word to the wounded Jew lying on the road to Jericho. He took practical means—transportation and personal expense—to see that the sufferer was comfortably installed where he could enjoy adequate care. St. Ignatius Loyola, founder of the Jesuits, was not content merely to lament the pitiful condition of unmarried mothers or young girls exposed to moral dangers in a big city: he built homes and obtained charity workers to look after them. St. Vincent de Paul was not satisfied with collecting alms for France's vast hordes of destitute victims of generations of war and poverty: he organized his relief, and suffered hard criticism for doing so. His great nineteenth-century follower, the saintly layman Frédéric Ozanam, founder of the Society of St. Vincent de Paul, declared bluntly that the love for neighbor was no genuine love unless it went to the roots of human misery and defended people's natural rights with the same generosity and strength that it expended in giving the more immediate relief.

It is not enough, says Pope Pius XI in his "Reconstruction" encyclical mentioned above, merely to practise "remedial charity." We need to practise "preventive charity" as well. Preventive charity will not be deceived by mere casual outward appearances. It will penetrate the deeper causes of human destitution and suffering. It will not hesitate to utilize the full machinery of modern sociological and psychological research, statistics and surveys, as long as these are sincerely conducted and are directed to an honest end. In the hands of Catholics, it will be expected to realize the full program of Catholic social welfare work, and will co-operate with constructive features of such work from whatever quarter. In the process of such an undertaking, it will naturally cope with the question of race relations and racial prejudice.

CHRIST OUR PEACE

Faith, as we have just seen, confirms the moral law as to man's natural dignity and the rights that flow from that dignity. Faith, we also saw, adds a *higher motive,* one of fraternal love; a special reason why we, as Christians, as followers of our Lord Jesus Christ and members of the Church that He founded, should treat all men as our brothers, since Christ our Lord died for all. All men have been redeemed by Jesus Christ and enjoy the same supernatural dignity and rights as either actual or possible members of His Mystical Body. In this great family, distinctions grounded upon race or nationality are expressly excluded. They were wiped out, obliterated by the Blood of the Redeemer who died for all mankind without distinction.

Jesus, says St. Paul, by His death upon the cross became "our

104

Peace." He broke down the wall of separation that heretofore had separated the race of Israel from the pagan world; separated the Jew from the Gentile. So important, so essential is this theme for the Christian idea that Jesus our Lord seemed to leave no stone unturned in order to enforce the lesson of the universal scope of the Kingdom He had come to found, using special imaginative appeal and emphasis, as in the parable of the Good Samaritan. He had come to save all men, and regarded them all with a universal love. Avoiding all unnecessary provocation, He nevertheless repeated the thesis directly in the face of the intense opposition it aroused among His listeners, who conceived the Kingdom of the Messias as offering the first place—spiritually and politically—to themselves as literal descendants of the patriarch Abraham. The Saviour insisted that the stranger and the foreigner would be welcomed and given equal honors in the Kingdom of Heaven.

Those leaders among the Jews, people who stubbornly refused to recognize the clear proofs that Jesus Christ offered in support of His own claim of divinity, found it easy to play upon the intensely nationalistic emotions and deep-rooted prejudices of the multitudes, embittered as these were by centuries of cruel oppression. The universal world scope of the Kingdom was depicted as a scandal. As a result, our Saviour's experience, the conflict between love and hate that raged around His sacred Person, parallels to an uncanny degree many an issue affecting interracial peace in our own day. Indeed, it is true for the whole world what Archbishop Owen McCann of Capetown, South Africa, recently said, that the attitude toward those of another race must be the attitude "that our Lord Jesus would take," and this, as the archbishop points out, applies to both parties in the conflict. Racial hatred and racial intolerance pander to that deadly enemy of our salvation, towering human pride.

THE MYSTERY OF BAPTISM

The Church that Christ established, in order to carry on His work through all space and time, was expressly to be for all human beings, without any exception whatsoever, and all would enter it upon equal terms, becoming through the grace of baptism members of the new, supernatural family or household of the Lord, just as they were already members of the great human family by their creation and common origin. This truth is beautifully expressed in the Church's various prayers that attend the celebration on Holy Saturday of the great Paschal Mystery; as for instance:

"O God, who art power unchangeable and light eternal: mercifully regard the wonderful mystery of Thy whole Church, and by an effect of Thy perpetual providence perform with tranquility the work of human salvation: and let the whole world experience and see that what is fallen is raised up, what was old is made new, and all things are re-established, through Him that gave them their first being, our Lord Jesus Christ Thy Son. . . ."

And in the Church's collect for the Feast of Christ the King (last Sunday of October):

"Almighty everlasting God, who in your beloved Son, King of the whole world, willed to restore all things anew; grant in your mercy that all the families of nations [*gentes,* races] rent asunder by the wound of sin, may be subjected to His most gentle rule."

In other words, He established the Catholic, the universal Church. The Church's catholicity was not meant to be a mere ornament or title, so called because *de facto* it contains people of many races and origins around the world. The Church's catholicity, like her holiness and her unity, is a dynamic attribute: something to be exemplified in every unit of the Church's life, and in the life of each one of her members. Hence, a parish is no longer a really Catholic parish in spirit if on the grounds of race it bans any people from its ministrations or treats them in matters that belong to the parish as minors or unequals.

When in 1942 the family of the late James J. Hoey established in his memory an annual award for two Catholic laymen, one Negro and one white, who had done outstanding work on behalf of interracial justice, the day chosen permanently for bestowing the medal was the Feast of Christ the King. On that day the Church recalls to our minds the union of all races and peoples in Christ's Kingdom here on earth, as they will be eventually united with Him in the Kingdom of His Father.

Deep wounds are not easily healed. But the Good Samaritan poured oil and wine into the wounds of the stranger who lay helpless on the road to Jericho, and set him on the road to recovery. Each one of us can go and do likewise.

THE EUCHARISTIC UNION

In no institution of the Catholic Church is the lesson of interracial justice and charity taught more profoundly than in the holy sacrifice of the Mass. It is unfortunate that this lesson has been so much ignored, so little understood.

The notion that the Eucharist is par excellence the sacrament of Catholic unity has been the constant doctrine of the Church. St. Thomas Aquinas calls it the "sacrament of ecclesiastical unity." The same thought reappears in the decrees of the Council of Trent and in the encyclicals of Pius X and Pius XII. Modern spiritual writers, however, have tended to overlook the social aspect of the Eucharist. As a result, the term "communion" for most Catholics today suggests only the union of the individual soul with Christ. As a corrective, it is stimulating to go back to the doctrine and practices of the primitive Church, which strikingly present the Eucharist as a source and sign of unity among the whole people of God.

The ancient practices of the Church give eloquent testimony to the dogmatic truth that the Eucharist is the sacrament of ecclesiastical unity. The same principle is inculcated, though not always by the same ceremonies, in the modern Roman liturgy. The kiss of peace, for example, now occupies a place immediately before the Communion, and is accompanied by a beautiful prayer for the peace and unity of the Church. A similar lesson is contained in many of the proper prayers, such as the Secret of the Mass of Corpus Christi, written by St. Thomas himself: "We beseech Thee, O Lord, mercifully grant to Thy Church the gifts of unity and peace, which are mystically signified beneath the gifts we offer."

In our own generation, as never before, there is need to demonstrate that Christianity is capable of bringing mankind into a truly universal society based not on fear and compulsion but on mutual love. To manifest the unitive power of Christian charity we must make faithful use of the means of unity which Christ has provided for His Church. Among these the Eucharist holds a place of honor as the supreme source and symbol of Catholic unity. Its true nature is eloquently expressed in the triple exclamation of St. Augustine, "O sacrament of affection. O sign of unity! O bond of charity!"

This great lesson of unity is gloriously symbolized through the sacramental species of bread and wine. The bread is made up of many grains baked together into one loaf. The wine is created out of many grapes. The grapes themselves, being the fruit springing from one vine, serve as a symbol. Jesus Himself developed this symbol with profound meaning and sentiment at His discourse on the eve of His crucifixion. "I am the Vine, you are its branches" (John 15:5). The Mass is the re-enactment of the cross's mighty onslaught upon human differences: the breaking down of the wall of partition. We participate in common, as in one family, in the holy Eucharistic offering. We are united with one another through our union with Jesus Christ in Communion. Each of these three approaches presents vast perspectives.

Many of these ideas we find symbolized in the ancient monuments of Christianity, in the windows and carvings of the ancient cathedrals. They are described in the writings of the Fathers of the Church, and again proclaimed in the Church's liturgy. At the conclusion of Holy Week all these ideas are united, brought back to their starting point in Baptism and swept forward to the glory of the Resurrection.

Hence it is that the study of the Church's Eucharistic doctrine or, more widely, of her complete sacramental doctrine—the whole mystery of the Redemption incarnate in space and time—is the most essential part of the Catholic faith. Jesus Christ, its Founder, at the time He performed His great redemptive act of sacrifice and love at a given moment in history, chose to perpetuate it among all men, everywhere, as a "clean oblation" offered to the Most High. Hence, this dynamic, outgoing love of the heart of Jesus for all men and all people and races is forever renewed in our midst through the sacrament and the sacrifice of the Holy Eucharist.

Speaking at the National Liturgical Conference in Worcester, Massachusetts, on August 28, 1955, Most Rev. Vincent S. Waters, Bishop of Raleigh, drew the obvious lesson:

"Catholics are united in a Christian social body by the greatest possible ties in the universe, the ties of the Mystical Body of Christ. We all understand how close are the ties of nature, between a mother and her children. Yet two persons in the Mystical Body, though they may be in opposite parts of the world and of diverse racial characteristics, are closer in the Mystical Body than a pagan mother and her own children. . . .

"Can we accuse and blame those of racial injustice who do not have the Mass? How can they learn to appreciate the unity if they do not have the Center of unity? Can we blame those for their racial injustice who have the Mass but do not understand it? Shall we not rather blame ourselves for not being more able to promote the liturgy—the understanding of the Mass? In the Mass we have a furnace of the love of God. There His brethren can be brought to a white heat of love and fused with each other as they are infused into Christ. That is why the Mass is so important."

LESSON OF THE MASS

Today the Church is emphasizing more and more the corporate nature of her official worship. The Mass is not only a public act of worship; it is also and eminently a corporate act of worship. Only once throughout the entire liturgy of the Mass—after the initial prayers at the foot of the altar—does the ministering priest speak in his own name, and that is when he prepares to make his own Communion at the consummation of the Holy Sacrifice. For the rest, it is priest and people, those present, for all the faithful, for the living and the dead—in a word, for the entire people of God. With them and for them, he prays and pleads and pledges. As St. Paul puts it, "You are all the children of God by faith in Christ Jesus. For as many of you as have been baptized in Christ have put on Christ. There is neither Jew nor Greek; there is neither bond nor free; there is neither male nor female. For you are all one in Christ Jesus."

Five times during the august celebration the priest turns toward the people with whom and in whose name he acts to remind of the unity of the people of God: *Dominus vobiscum; Orate fratres.*

"Holy Mass is a national act of worship," writes Monsignor Wilson, of Jamaica, British West Indies, "for the cross of Christ has created a new nation of men. This divine race will continue to live within the shadow of that cross which is perpetually represented and represented from millions of Catholic altars. This new nation, this sturdy race is unique in the history of mankind. It is a race created not by blood, but by grace. It is a nation whose boundaries are not determined by geographical lines or linguistic affinities, but by a common profession of faith. If we realize the intimate bonds which unite priest and people and the Victim and the Godhead before the holy altar, we will find strength and courage and grace. We will be able to fulfil in ourselves 'what is wanting in the Passion of Christ.' How great is the need of our modern world for such participation!

"Some 15,000,000 American Negroes are seeking their share in these treasures of God's bounty. They know the bitterness of human sacrifices on the demands of human greed and inhuman indifference. They dread a sacrifice that brings death, not life. They know of the divine democracy of Christ. They should belong to the new race; to the people of God. Christ has offered and is offering Himself daily—nay, hourly—for all mankind. He is offering Himself for them. Christ is our Brother. He is their Brother. Mary is our Mother. She is their Mother. God is our Father. He is their Father. They are legitimate heirs *de jure* of Heaven. They need the Mass. They must have the Mass.

"Holy Mass also promotes the attainment of social justice for the whole racial group. Besides, the Catholic understands that Holy Mass is the same as the sacrifice of Calvary, the idea of justice is continually before his eyes. The cross of Calvary is the payment of man's debt to God and every time Holy Mass is celebrated, this idea of justice is brought back to mind. The constant remembrance of our duty to God helps us to fulfil the duty to our fellow men. Thus it is that the Mass prompts and aids and enlivens our work in bringing into possession of their rightful heritage 15,000,000 American Negroes with souls as precious as our own and for whom no less than for us the drama of Calvary continues."*

THE CHRISTIAN'S TASK

From the standpoint of doctrinal approach to the problems of racial relations two major tasks, therefore, await the Christian.

The first is to increase the *knowledge* in our own minds and in those of our neighbors, the knowledge of what it really means to be a Catholic, to be a member of the truly universal Church. We need more diffusion of knowledge, more theology, both as to the nature of the Church itself and to the profound meaning of the Holy Eucharist and the Eucharistic community, as touched upon in these recent quotations.†

The second task is the actual implementing of that knowledge in our relation to our neighbor. I am not thinking so much of an anxious collection of individual acts as of the formation

---

* Right Rev. Gladstone O. Wilson, "The Mass and Interracial Justice," *Interracial Review*, February, 1940, pp. 28–29.
† The encyclical *Mystici Corporis* (On the Mystical Body of Christ) by Pope Pius XII is a masterly exposition of this subject (English translation, America Press, 70 E. 45th St., New York 17, N. Y.) and of a work like *Catholicism*, by Henri di Lubac, S.J. (Longmans, Green, 1950), will help to enlighten us on this point.

in our hearts of a genuinely Catholic attitude, which will manifest itself in countless ways. From this vantage point we shall be inspired—according to the classic formula of Catholic Action—to *inquire* intelligently, painstakingly, and impartially into the scene around us and all its many factors; to make up our minds, *judge,* and so reach real practical decisions, regardless of what they may cost us; and, finally, to *act* upon what we have decided.

Where, therefore, strong temptations to discrimination, where differences occur, as may be the case in a rapidly changing neighborhood on the arrival of new peoples and strangers, precisely in *such* instances does the spirit of true Catholicity need to come into play. It is precisely then, under such circumstances, that the Catholic shows himself or herself, no longer just a Catholic in name, or a Catholic in official registration or affiliation, but a Catholic in deed and truth; effectively and genuinely Catholic, according to the mind of Christ and of His Church.

Such dynamic, whole-souled Catholicity is easier to talk about than to practise. In many cases it would be quite beyond our strength if we were left to our own unaided reserves of courage and charity. Here again our faith comes to our aid with the living power and intimate companionship of the Redeemer.

Deeds, not words, was the blunt formula of the heroic apostle of the slaves, St. Peter Claver of Cartagena. It is the deeds, not the words, that will be recorded in the day of judgment. However—lest it be misunderstood—in a vast number of cases the *right words,* cast like seed upon the wide field of human opinion, are themselves fruitful of deeds. Jesus Christ promised the reward at the last judgment to those who did deeds of mercy for the least of His brethren. And He also promised honor and glory to those who, fearless of the opinions and threats of other human beings, will boldly confess His holy name. By words and by deeds of mercy, justice, and truth we confess the name of Him who is the Author of peace and the Hope of all nations of the world.

PART IV

What the Individual Can Do

A. AS AN INDIVIDUAL

First of all, it is important to realize that one *can* do something about it. There is nothing more fatal and absurd than the notion of inevitable, unbreakable patterns of prejudice and discrimination. As we have already seen, racial prejudice is itself not inborn; it is acquired: acquired, it is true, early in childhood, imperceptibly, but nevertheless not as a necessary trait of our nature. The problem as such is not insoluble. On the contrary, experience surprisingly shows how much can be accomplished with comparatively little effort by willing hearts and minds. We discover how fruitful and how rewarding is any effort in this direction, if it is undertaken in an intelligent fashion with a humble understanding of one's own limitations and a clear picture of just what we are trying to accomplish here and now.

The primary question, in the order of any practical action, is not so much to convert the hard core of intractable, stubborn minds as to lay the truth before the great multitude of honest, sincere people wherever they may live or whatever may be their circumstances. So many people are uncertain, apathetic or confused. With regard to the racial situation, it is much the same as with regard to the Christian faith itself: people welcome a sane and just view if it is properly put and clearly explained.

Our effort, however, must be consistent. It is just as reprehensible to practise a racism in reverse as it is to show the more familiar type of racial prejudice. The individual must lay aside not only his dislike of people of another culture or appearance but his own sensitiveness and clannishness as well.

SIMPLEST METHODS BEST

In matters where human emotions are concerned the simplest methods are often the best. Great progress is often achieved when people know that there *is* a Catholic position on the question of race relations. This proposition may seem simple enough to one who has read the preceding pages, but it surprises many people. They are astonished that Christianity sets standards of right or wrong in our dealings with our neighbor, just as many people are astonished that the Church sets standards of right or wrong in business practices. For many it is a new idea that their treatment of their neighbor is actually a matter of conscience, whether it be on the line of business transactions or in the question of racial attitudes.

People, too, are surprised to find that social conformity is not the last word. The Church has always taught a decent respect for traditions in the secular world and observed them in her own life. But this is entirely different from letting society tyrannize over our moral and our spiritual life. Social conformity has taken charge when an otherwise good Christian, suddenly confronted with his duty toward his neighbor or another race or culture, takes refuge in the assertion. This is the way people feel or think in our community; so what can you do about it?

Were mere social conformity generally to govern our religious life it would create anarchy. As Catholics, for instance, we are obliged to practise a certain amount of social nonconformity. Our marriage laws, the Church's precepts on attendance at Mass and the religious education of our children and other requirements of our faith bring us in conflict with the common usage of the community around us. Hence, there is no point in a Catholic's appealing to mere social practices as a final arbiter.

When it comes to asserting either our faith or the principles that are drawn from our faith, certain concrete situations call for a degree of independence in our attitudes. When, for instance, in conversation among a group of people we have to listen to a flagrant misstatement with regard to the racial question, there is certainly an obligation to take some action on our part. It is time quietly but firmly to argue our neighbor, as best we can, out of that false position. We do not gain by thrusting arguments down a person's throat. We only prejudice our own cause if we attempt to do so. St. Paul (Rom. 10:2) rebukes those people "who have zeal of God, but not according to knowledge." Where feelings are so strong and subjective convictions are tenacious, it is most important that we show a respect for the other person's point of view. We assume in every case that our dissenters are sincere and we do not accuse them of acting from unreason and passion. Nevertheless, we need to remind them that there is a basic teaching on this matter and we should be able to sum up that teaching in a few words, as we have explained in the preceding chapters.

SOME ANOMALIES

Apart from questions of fundamental religious principle, ordinary common sense will often show prejudiced people how mistaken is their point of view. It is an anomaly, for instance, that in a democracy like ours a newly landed immigrant in this country who has been with us only a few hours has more civil rights to his credit, even though still an alien, than one whose citizenship is rooted for several generations back. Yet an American citizen, a product of our schools, our culture, our entire United States civilization, an old American, in a very true sense, must still struggle for elementary rights, simply because he is identified in the popular mind with people who were once in a condition of servitude.

Racial prejudice, as it is, is the source of any number of curious inconsistencies. It is anomalous, for instance, that in our big cities we think nothing of living next door, possibly in the same apartment house, to persons whose family life is completely reprehensible according to our Catholic or Christian standards, as long as they do not molest us personally. Yet we become acutely disturbed at the presence of a well-bred, educated, law-abiding, neighborly family, merely because of the color of their skin. Many people have not reflected on these strange inconsistencies any more than they reflect on the anomaly of trying, in our present-day conditions, to confine any one group of people permanently to the servant class.

The statement that a member of a certain racial group is all right if he is kept "in his place" is one of the many popular slogans which we need to challenge directly by showing how fallacious they are under closer examination. We need only ask a person: If the Negro or any other type of citizen needs to be kept in his place, what is that place and please define it? If it means that people who have not yet attained a certain degree of culture must put up with the consequences of their own backwardness, we can naturally agree. But it is entirely illogical if it means that they are to be permanently consigned to an inferior status regardless of what degree of culture they may have attained. It is contrary to the entire tradition of American democracy to hold, even implicitly, that persons should be discouraged from emerging from a lower degree of culture or from developing the talents which they have received from the Creator. Such a notion is likewise contrary to the principle of intellectual integrity which we saw as a fundamental in our Catholic teaching on the human person.

STATUS OF SERVANT

To repudiate the notion of a compulsory and permanent servant status is not to be falsely understood as a reflection on the idea of personal service as a chosen form of occupation. The servant status of itself can be both profitable and noble. A person can represent human dignity in the status of a domestic servant quite as much as in any other career in life. Christ Himself, says St. Paul, took on the form of a servant, even of a slave; and the Pope's highest title is "Servant of the servants of God." Domestic or personal service is simply one of the many careers or vocations which a person can choose, and a very honorable one. But choosing such a status voluntarily, according to one's own personal liking, is entirely different from being consigned to it as something necessarily attached to one's origin or one's physical condition. Indeed, some of the unreasonable prejudice that housewives complain they find against the status of domestic service in this country, the extreme unwillingness of many people to engage in domestic service who might be quite happy therein, has come precisely from this false point of view, the feeling that you are being permanently identified with a certain status if you engage in a servant's career.

Whatever be the popular tenets on this point, the time has passed when any group of people will remain content with being assigned to a certain inferior status in our American democracy or, in fact, anywhere in the world. It is only wishful thinking to imagine that day can be prolonged or to blame others for being unwilling to try to prolong it.

Similar plain speaking is in order where within our own community, say, for instance, within the parish community, gossip has arisen with regard to recent arrivals. It is easy to create alarm among anxious, timid souls by the announcement that people of other races have entered the parish, are now being seen in church, may possibly sit in a pew next to us, etc. But objections raised on this point are completely contrary to the spirit of the Church itself. The Church has never excluded the poor. She has always welcomed all to her house without reservation, whether they are rich or poor, wise or foolish. A homogeneous, hand-picked congregation where people are mutually conformable in all their minor social ways is agreeable. It makes parish life smoother. But to require such conformity is entirely un-Catholic; it is contrary not only to the spirit of the Catholic Church in general, but to the tradition of the Catholic Church in the United States. If our ancestors in the past had encountered such an attitude, how few of them would have been able to maintain the faith. Today, with the mixture of many peoples and the constant shifts of population, there is the opportunity to show, vigorously and concretely, the *real* character of the Church, its true Catholicism.

SHOWING REAL CATHOLICISM

Happily, that real character does emerge; often, most unexpectedly.

Not a colored person attended the Catholic Church in Tullahoma, Tennessee. For many a Negro this would have seemed

ample reason for feeling some timidity about appearing there
on a Sunday morning. But it was not a reason that convinced
Private Clifford Sharp. This young soldier, former assistant
scoutmaster and assistant director of athletics in Holy Trinity
parish, Cincinnati, had as few misgivings about his fellow Catholics, wherever they might be found, as he had about the service of his country. When he was stationed at Tullahoma, and
phoned the pastor, a Paulist priest, asking about Mass, he obtained an immediate and cordial response. He received an
equally hearty welcome from the parishioners, who spoke to
him after the service and remarked about his devout assistance
at Mass. The long and short of it, as related in *Mission Fields
at Home,* published by the Sisters of the Blessed Sacrament,
was to find on the fourth Sunday a large sign on the front door
with a very cordial invitation to all colored people in the neighborhood to attend Mass at that church if they wished, and also
to take part in a regular course on Catholic doctrine.

There have been experiences of quite another caliber too
frequently for us to expect every Negro Catholic soldier to
share the courage and optimism of Private Sharp. For the timid
as well as for the confident, the path to the church door must be
smoothed, if souls are not to be lost by the wayside. But the
existence of men like Private Sharp, of pastors and congregations like those at Tullahoma, is an inspiration for all concerned.
And the story should hearten many a Negro Catholic soldier
to take a good long chance in exploring the opportunities to
practise his religion, regardless of any local traditions.

EIGHT SUGGESTIONS

In a very practical little pamphlet, *The Catholic Church and
Race Relations* (published by The America Press), two apos-

tolic priests of the archdiocese of Newark, New Jersey—Fathers
Edward J. Hayes and Paul J. Hayes—offer "out of many that
might be advanced" the following simple suggestions on what
one can personally do.

(1) Be active in your own parish and your own church organization, by working patiently and tactfully for the promo-
tion of fully Catholic policies.

(2) Become acquainted with the priests and the Sisters engaged in work for the Negro, and do what you can to assist
them and make their work better known.

(3) Assist worthy and talented and qualified colored young
folk of either sex to obtain a good education, by contributing
to scholarships or otherwise. Sometimes, you may find yourself
assisting a priestly or religious vocation.

(4) Write a letter occasionally to your diocesan press [or to
the general daily press] praising what is good, giving notice of
fine personal achievements, or calling attention to any serious
injustice. Any such communication, however, should be scru-
pulously truthful, and as fair and as constructive as possible.

(5) Try to learn of conditions in your own immediate neighborhood, and be willing to co-operate in honest and approved
efforts for their betterment.

(6) Encourage the work of interracial college and alumni
groups.

(7) Form a contact with the Catholic Interracial Council, if
one of these is organized in your city.

(8) If you live in the South, become acquainted with the
Commission on Human Rights of the Catholic Committee of
the South, from which valuable advice and material may be
obtained (Box 694, New Orleans, Louisiana).

(9) Finally, pray daily for the great intentions urged by the
Pope, and pray constantly in union with the Saviour's prayer
that all men may be one, as He and His Father are one.

LIKES AND DISLIKES

Human conduct, as I have remarked elsewhere,* can never be a matter of mere clever adjustment. Man can hardly live without a certain degree of tension. Indeed, a society without any tensions whatsoever would—short of Heaven—seem to be a lifeless society. The nobler, the more sensitive, the more responsible and conscientious people are, the more they suffer from the peculiarities of their neighbors. We cannot help feeling strong likes and dislikes. The problem is not to become devoid of feeling, for such would not be human, but to avoid being mastered by it: of letting it rule our own decisions. It is not easy to control these feelings, to repress instinctive reactions to other peoples' ignorance, selfishness, importunity, irresponsibility. It is hard for the precise, deliberate and industrious person to live and keep house side by side with careless, haphazard neighbors.

This is not meant as a plea for tolerating such unneighborly faults as faults; still less for excusing them, in ourselves or in others. Where such misconduct exists in the community, it is obviously our right and duty to leave no stone unturned in order to be rid of it. But it is a plea for a rational, practical approach to the problem, for a treatment of the neighbor that will respect his personality, win him over to the good, and enlist him as a partner in a common search for a better community and—in the words of Father Riccardo Lombardi, S.J., Italy's apostle of dynamic charity and social wisdom—"for a better world," *per un mondo migliore.*

Hence it is that in the conflict of racial attitudes we fre-

* "The Basis of Interracial Peace," *Voice of St. Jude,* December, 1954.

quently arrive at a point where we need to ask ourselves: How does my reaction in this particular instance agree with the whole Christian tradition on justice and mutual responsibility? Someone somewhere has to make a sacrifice; we cannot make this demand all one-sided. In the vast majority of cases a sacrifice has to be made by both parties to the difficulty.

In the case of a Negro or other minority-group member moving into a white neighborhood, the white person has to sacrifice his own desire for a completely homogeneous neighborhood in order to do justice to his neighbor, for his neighbor has a genuine right in ethics and in our American society to occupy a home for himself and family. On the other hand, the member of the minority group cannot dispense himself from making the necessary and very strenuous effort to conform to decent living standards and to accommodate himself to the reasonable wishes of his neighbors; to be, in the full sense of the word, a *good,* constructive, helpful neighbor. Such truly neighborly conduct on everybody's part is a matter of conscience, and there can be no interracial peace without the formation of an interracial conscience all around.

WHAT PARENTS CAN DO

Parents can do much to help their children develop more positive racial attitudes and make a more effective adjustment to the present rapid changes in race relations. Dr. Kenneth B. Clark, in his thoughtful little book of advice to both white and Negro parents,* makes the first requirement for a well-intentioned parent that he exercise control over expressions of his

* *Prejudice and Your Child* (Boston, The Beacon Press, 1956), pp. 128–129.

own racial feelings. It's not helping his children to use in their presence vulgar epithets for people of other races or religions, and it is not preparing them to function effectively in the modern world.

The parent, too, should not be afraid to discuss his own prejudice frankly with his own children. "Since it is the responsibility of parents to provide basic moral and ethical guidance for their children," says Dr. Clark, "white parents are almost obliged to deal with the moral, ethical and religious implications of racial prejudice."

"A parent who believes in the religious principle of the brotherhood of man and the fatherhood of God, a parent who accepts the American democratic creed, should under no circumstances punish his child for favorable expressions of racial democracy." Parents should set up no special standards and, at the same time, make "no special allowances in intelligence, behavior, or cleanliness for the Negro friend if they would not do the same for other children." A well-intentioned white parent can set an example for children by the nature and quality of his own relationships with individuals of other groups. "He can make them realize, just as he has learned to realize himself, that there is a wide range of individual differences among Negroes as there is among other people." There are always plenty of people whom we find unsympathetic, plenty of people whom we simply cannot like. The point is that in so many cases we can learn to like those whom we previously disliked. And even if we cannot change our instinctive sentiments, our deliberate conduct toward others should be guided by what people genuinely are, not by their outward appearance or racial accident.

THE MARRIAGE QUESTION

The difficulty is sometimes raised: Will not friendly association between the races lead to intermarriage?

I have previously written at length* that I have found no evidence to the effect that the establishment of friendly, just and charitable relations between the Negro and white groups encourages any notable tendency to intermarriage. Indications seemed to point in the contrary direction: that in proportion as the pressure of fear and insecurity is removed from the minority group and its status raised by education and improved welfare, spiritual and temporal, the better opportunity is offered to its youth to find suitable life partners with its own numbers.

In point of fact, marriage with those of another race does not appear to be a matter of predominant interest to the vast majority of Negroes.

As for the rights and wrongs in this matter, no scientific proof appears to be available as to deleterious effects, from a purely biological standpoint, of the union between different races of mankind, despite various popular legends. Much of what is termed racial intermarriage is between persons who, on at least one side of the marriage, are already of mixed race.

As for the moral aspect, in the first place, there can be no such thing, from a moral point of view, as compulsory friendly association. Every human being, the Negro included, has a right to choose and select his close, personal friends and associates.

In the second place, the Catholic Church does not impose

* *The Race Question and the Negro* (New York, Longmans, 1943), pp. 192–199.

any impediment upon racial intermarriages, in spite of the Church's great care to preserve in its utmost purity the integrity of the marriage bond. And she safeguards the right of persons to choose their own marriage partners, so long as they observe the laws that the Church considers essential to the integrity of the sacrament of matrimony. However, from a purely prudential standpoint, serious reasons can militate against entering into such a marriage, where—as is very apt to be the case—there is a wide difference between the parties as to their social background or social environment. This is particularly the case in sections of the country where racial differences have become rigidly crystallized by custom and tradition.*

B.   THROUGH ORGANIZED ACTION

We have so far discussed largely the question of individual action, but the inquiry is also raised to what the individual may accomplish by means of organized action. No extensive goal can be attained without the systematic collaboration of others.

The first work of any organized group is that of study. It is better for a group devoting itself to the problem of race relations to be well informed even if inactive than to be highly active but badly informed. Hence, any organized group should take ample time out before engaging in active programs—several months at least, or a year—to prepare themselves and should continue this self-preparation in some form or other permanently throughout their work. They can never be too well informed. Such information turns chiefly on three main points.

* For a more detailed treatment of this matter, see Appendix A.

LEARNING THE FACTS

First of all, we need to grasp firmly the fundamental principles in the whole question, such as already have been discussed: principles drawn from our religious faith, from the applications of that faith in the Catholic Church; principles also of our own Government, such as the rights and duties of the citizen in a democratic regime.

In the second place, we need a general knowledge of the facts, some idea of the main facts of history, the story of the minority group and its efforts at self-advancement and at self-liberation; its successes and failures, as well as the co-operation it has received from its friends. We need to know something of the sociological data at the present time; something about the distribution of the different races, their actual condition, economic, social, or religious. Even in dealing with purely local questions it is of immense help to have a general sociological background.

In the third place, we naturally wish to acquaint ourselves with the particular facts of the locality in which we live: its principal personalities, the tensions and strains in the community, the problems of adjustment as they have been felt in recent times. We need to be informed as to the aims, personnel, and procedure of the organizations active in the field; in other words, to be fully familiar with the environment in which we are working.

Above all, nothing is more important than to keep always clear before our minds that in dealing with these questions we are dealing not with an abstract entity known as race, but with living persons: with their concerns, interests (spiritual and physical), ambitions, virtues, and faults.

What the Individual Can Do

Our study project can be fitted into the framework of the parish, as an enterprise of one of the parish organizations, or as a distinct study group organized for this purpose in the parish; or it can be based on an interparochial or diocesan plan in connection with social activities of the diocese, such as the Sodality of the Blessed Virgin, the Legion of Mary, the Holy Name Society, the various Catholic Action groups. It can profitably be conducted with the schools as an activity, particularly on the high-school as well as on the college and university level, and suggestions are available on this point.

SOURCES OF KNOWLEDGE

An immense amount of practical information, especially as to action in the Southern region of the United States, can be obtained from the Catholic Committee of the South (P.O. Box 982, Rock Hill, South Carolina). This vibrant group of priests and laymen under episcopal direction promotes the full life of the Mystical Body of Christ. It seeks to correct false concepts of social order and to inculcate the principles outlined in the papal encyclicals. It encourages a vital, Catholic faith which by the impact of example, education, and direct action will influence an ever-widening circle.

The idea of the Catholic Committee of the South was conceived in 1939, and the organization came into being at Atlanta, Georgia, in the spring of 1940, at a convention attended by bishops, priests, Sisters and laymen. A specific program was drawn up, planning, among other things, "to bring about a Christian understanding among Southerners, irrespective of race or creed." The ordinaries and auxiliary bishops of the dioceses involved formed the board of governers. The executive board consists of four bishops, with a priest as general chairman and a layman as vice chairman. There are six general departments—race relations, labor and industry, education, rural life, the Southern apostolate, and youth. Linked with their work is the Institute of Industrial Relations at Loyola University of the South, directed by Rev. Louis J. Twomey, S.J., open to persons of all ages and classes, both white and Negro. The unique "Think Groups," which originated in the diocese of Alexandria, are small groups of men carefully selected for leadership ability and knowledge of social problems.

FRIENDSHIP HOUSE

Friendship House is an interracial lay apostolate devoted to the sanctification of its members and the social environment in which they live. It has been primarily concerned with interracial justice since 1938, when its foundress, Baroness Catherine de Hueck, established the Harlem Friendship House in New York City. Other Friendship Houses are now located in segregated Negro sections of Chicago, Washington, D.C., and Portland, Oregon.

The movement has a twofold purpose: educational work to correct the prejudices which cause racial discrimination, and social service effort to alleviate the hardships which Negroes suffer as a result of segregation and discrimination. Its work in the Negro community includes youth programs, adult classes, libraries, reading rooms, forums, emergency assistance, and clothing distribution.

The work of Friendship House is carried on by full-time staff members and by part-time volunteers. The staff workers practise the virtues of poverty, charity, and obedience, but not under the discipline of vows. Daily Mass and Communion, and spiritual exercises, are part of their community life. They work without compensation other than a nominal monthly allowance for personal necessities. They are dependent on charity for their clothing.

Friendship House publishes a monthly newspaper, *Community*. The present national director of the movement is Miss Anne Foley, whose address is 4233 South Indiana Avenue, Chicago 15, Illinois.

CURRENT INFORMATION

Essential to any fruitful study is the knowledge of the many practical methods by which people of different origins and cultures can learn to know one another. We should be equipped with the answers to popular slogans, abounding in the field of human relations and in the field of politics, where they are often more potent than elaborate arguments.* *Interracial Review*, a monthly published by the Catholic Interracial Council (20 Vesey St., New York 7, N.Y.), supplies a steady service of current information and documentation. Simple, practical suggestions are offered in Lillian Smith's *The Time is Now*. Miss Smith, a white Southerner, writes from practical experience. She is particularly helpful in analyzing many of the current slogans that help to confuse minds and excite passions.

Much good can be done by an occasional letter to the press praising some fine utterance or deed that may help to create better understanding, or to business firms or to hospitals commending them for examples of fair racial practices—or even by a well-placed phone call.

* Many of these were discussed in the author's own work, *The Race Question and the Negro*, Chapter 24.

PERSONAL CONTACTS

Information gained from written sources needs to be supplemented by personal contact, by consultation with qualified persons who can speak directly from first-hand knowledge—whether it be in the form of a formal lecture, followed preferably by questions and answers, or in the more familiar fashion of simple offhand conversations. Direct contact with other persons, with other experiences, is more illuminating than much that one can learn from books. Such contacts can be arranged readily through local or state interracial agencies as well as through a local Catholic Interracial Council. PTA groups—white or colored—local Chambers of Commerce, and various public discussion groups can be most helpful. Difficulties that seem most alarming to the casual point of view, such as the question of the possibility of intermarriage, turn out to be easily soluble when looked at under the analysis of Christian principle.*

WORK OF THE COUNCILS

In cities where the Catholic Interracial Council is already organized, ample information can be obtained and opportunities offered for collaboration with their work. Councils differ in organization from place to place, but all follow the same general principle of an educational and co-operative approach to the racial problem. They exist as of January 1, 1956, in the following cities: New York, Brooklyn, Philadelphia, Detroit, Chicago,

* See also Appendix A.

Chicago West Suburban, St. Louis, Baltimore, Washington, D.C., Wilmington, Columbus, Saginaw, Syracuse, Indianapolis, Hartford, New Haven, Providence, Bakersfield (Cal.), Pittsburgh, Richmond, San Antonio, New Orleans, Lafayette (La.), Greensboro, Raleigh, Charlotte, Durham, and Rock Hill (S.C.).

The last nine mentioned are in the Southern states. The New Orleans Council is known as the Commission on Human Rights, of the Catholic Committee of the South. Other councils are in process of formation in various parts of the United States, and inquiries have been received from abroad as to the possibility of establishing Catholic Interracial Councils in other countries.

Interracial Councils "are a source of immense good," in a field where there is "real need for Catholic Action," Archbishop Amleto Giovanni Cicognani, Apostolic Delegate to the United States, told members of the Washington Council on December 17, 1946. "Through discussions," he said, "you create a common sentiment, you promote social relations on the basis of Christian principles, you lend your own co-operation to eliminate lamentable discriminations, and you open avenues for progress: spiritual, educational and even material."

The Negro apostolate would be aided by the establishment of Catholic Interracial Councils in more dioceses, Right Rev. Cornelius J. Drew, pastor of the Harlem parish of St. Charles Borromeo, declared in a New York address on November 21, 1954. Much good will accrue to the Church as a result of Catholic social action, Monsignor Drew said.

"Catholic Interracial Councils are working to remedy a wrong by putting religious principles into effect. Down deep your motive is the fact that another person's soul is as dear to God as your own.

"We priests haven't the daily elbow-rubbing contact with the laity which you have. Negroes with whom you have daily contact know that you have come into this work because as Catholics you believe in the dignity of souls created to God's image. The fact that Catholics are interested in them for religious reasons is a new angle to many Negroes who have heard strange and unflattering things about the Church."

Discussing the problem of combating prejudice, Hon. Elmer A. Carter, member of the New York State Commission against Discrimination (a non-Catholic), declared:

"I know of no organization which is serving our country more nobly in this respect than the Catholic Interracial Council. Without fanfare throughout the years of its existence it has penetrated into the recesses of racial prejudice in schools and colleges and other areas of human activity and has replaced fear with confidence and antipathy with understanding and respect. It has brought to thousands of young men and women a realization of the teachings of their Church and their responsibility to their fellow-men."

Addressing the board of directors of the Catholic Interracial Council of Chicago on September 7, 1955, Samuel Cardinal Stritch, Archbishop of Chicago, stated frankly: "What a blessing it is for a bishop to have a group like this to help him in work. . . . I look upon you as one of the groups of lay apostles whom God in His goodness has gathered around me."

The author wrote in this connection some years ago: "Someone may exclaim: 'Yes, this is true, as to *what* should be done, but *how* is it to be accomplished?' Today, this 'how'? is answered, definitely and conclusively, by the establishment of the Catholic Interracial Councils. The work of the councils is a planned strategic attack upon our mightiest enemy, which is not as a rule human malice—for most men are not malicious— nor human violence, but a simple lack of information and the indifference or apathy that results from this uninformed state."*

---

* "A Call for Catholic Interracial Councils," *Interracial Review*, December, 1948, pp. 182–183.

A like diagnosis was made by the late Dr. John Hope, first president of Atlanta University, as the result of his endeavors to interest people in the education of his own race. The bitterest experience a worker in that cause could have, said Dr. Hope, "is not that of meeting doubt, despondency or hostility, but of coming in contact with bland, polite indifference." And he found, in spite of signs to the contrary, "a leaven of charity, a deep righteousness, and a belief in the American idea of rights and liberty" stretching far and wide among the American people.

Experience of nearly fifteen years has revealed to workers in the Catholic interracial cause the remarkable effectiveness and practicality of Catholic Interracial Councils. Such councils are set up as a joint project of representative men and women of different races. They maintain friendly, co-operative relations with similar-minded men and women of other religious bodies. The only condition is that their friends shall share their respect for the basic principles of morality and justice, founded upon the law of God. The councils conduct a widespread and varied educational program, using well-tried methods. They take a clear, thoroughly considered and firm stand on public matters that involve interracial justice and interracial good relations. They seek to promote such good relations in the religious community, that is to say in the life of the Church itself, with its various organizations and institutions. They seek to do the same also for the civic community, of which we all form a part.

The nature of the present world crisis calls for this work now. We have waited all too long and have too greatly imperiled the standing of our country abroad with our delays and evasions on basic racial questions. Some years ago I talked to a clever young Northern businessman, who prides himself on his culture, yet was shocked that Yale's football team had chosen a Negro, Levi Jackson, as its captain. Such a mind, with all its outward trappings of modernity and elegance, is completely out of tune with the real world as our diplomats, our delegates to the United Nations, our missionaries, our genuine statesmen know it. Some things may not be palatable for prejudiced minds, but the world is not built of pleasant tastes. Those who live, racially speaking, in a fool's paradise will one day suffer from a painfully rude awakening.

SOME CONCLUSIONS

The following are some conclusions adopted by a regional conference of several councils, as essential for their work:

(1) There is always plenty of work to do. Even when notorious abuses have been corrected, there remains a constant job of integration and consolidation.

(2) Each council should take pains to work close to its own bishop: interpret to him its work, anticipate his interests, and seek his counsel. The status of the New York office should always be kept clear: as a service center for all the councils, not a top bureau.

(3) Every place needs an occasional or a periodical event—religious or civic—to dramatize the interracial work, the problems it deals with and the remedies it proposes for them.

(4) This is not a work *by* one group *for* another. It is work done by all; a joint labor is one of the most precious fruits of the Council, working for something in which we are all interested.

(5) It is work *in* the general community, both civic and religious. Hence, the council's work should always be reaching out into the larger community, making a point of reaching the top levels, in business, labor, journalism, parish and diocesan activities, education, social work and social welfare, legislation,

etc. Though strictly non-political, we cannot be indifferent to political measures or attitudes that violate justice and charity.

(6) It is work for *all* the community, not just for one or the other disadvantaged group, not just for the peace of soul of the majority group. We need continually to emphasize our *common interest.*

(7) This point can be concretely brought out in such matters as the welfare of families, health, etc. In time of war mobilization, the manpower question needs to be emphasized. We attack segregation as a social policy not only on moral and Catholic grounds, but also because in itself it is a wasteful, expensive procedure, growing more so day by day.

(8) We want always to keep our Catholic integrity. The inner life of the council would suffer if we were to admit non-Catholics to membership. The same principle applies here as would, e.g., to the Jocist (Young Catholic Workers) movement. But we can and should co-operate generously with non-Catholics of good will in our outward relations: inviting them to consult with us on our plans, working with them on committees that bear real fruit. We are an "open," not a "closed," Catholic organization.

We co-operate with them *on two levels:* on the purely *civic* or "welfare" level, e.g., with regard to techniques, and on the higher *moral* level of the common defense of fundamental spiritual values. "Every Christian," said Pope Pius XII, "shall co-operate in giving back to the human person the dignity given it by God from the beginning . . . It is a fight for the human race which is gravely ill."[*]

Obviously, we do not co-operate in any shape or fashion with communists or "party liners." Where we are asked to join with committees that we suspect might have questionable pur-

[*] Christmas Message, 1952, NCWC ed., pp. 15–22.

poses or include questionable personalities, we insist that we be in on the plans for the committee and take nothing handed out to us ready-made.

(9) Last, but not least, we need always to keep in mind that our work is an apostolic, thoroughly supernatural work. For this reason it needs to be continually supported by fervent prayer and union with the Redeemer in the holy sacrifice of the Mass. Upon our own personal lives and sacrifice depends, in the last analysis, all that we can hope to accomplish.*

CATHOLIC ORGANIZATIONS

The same principle applies in the case of nation-wide Catholic organizations open to all persons who fulfil certain obvious requirements of religious practice and public and private morality, as long as they show sufficient good will and provide the required financial contributions. Where we find such organizations excluding men or women (as the case may be) from their membership not because of lack of qualifications according to the respective rules or constitutions of the order, but because of purely racial considerations, it is our duty to challenge such an un-Catholic attitude. The greater part of our national Catholic organizations in the United States have shown themselves remarkably consistent in the best sense of the word on this matter. In the last few years barriers have rapidly collapsed and American Catholics can be proud of a growing record of fairness and equity in our schools and in our national diocesan and local organizations. There remain, however, a few glaring exceptions. Certainly, nothing could be more deplorable than to see local units of a large and honored fraternal organization still practising purely racial exclusion.

* *Interracial Review*, March, 1951, pp. 43–44.

SECULAR ORGANIZATIONS

Our information will include familiarity with the aims and activities of some of the principal secular organizations working in this field. It is important to know their local activities, persons engaged in them and the projects in which they are active. It is equally important to be familiar with the over-all aims of the national or parent body. Through them a vast wealth of material is obtainable and they usually are ready to co-operate along their own lines. Outstanding in this respect are such national organizations as the National Association for the Advancement of Colored People (NAACP) which works through 1,300 chapters in forty-three states, the District of Columbia, and Alaska, for the vindication of civil rights for all people through strictly legal and constitutional means. The association describes the main objectives as:

(1) Using the courts to obtain justice under existing laws and fight abuses of the law;

(2) Seeking new national, and local laws to ban discrimination and protect civil rights;

(3) Promoting a climate of brotherhood through meetings, example, publications, and other educational media.

Also most helpful is the National Urban League, which is concerned with the problems of social adjustment in urban communities where questions of housing, employment, social welfare, etc., are affected by racial discrimination. Helpful also are various community organizations, state and municipal commissions, interracial commissions, such as the New York State Commission against Discrimination or the Minnesota State Commission on Race Relations. It is not possible in the compass of these few chapters to evaluate these organizations with their manifold operations and their many personalities. My recommendation is that the individual should not judge of them by mere hearsay, but shall approach them with an open mind, obtaining such information as is possible about their aims, methods, literature. Troublemakers—whether white or colored—whether of the noisy and bullying variety, or the underhand, secretive and scheming type, need to be kept in their place or at least avoided.

COMMUNIST AGENCIES

Such organizations as those already mentioned are to be clearly differentiated from various communist front groups which have proliferated in the past. A few are still fairly active in different parts of the country. Instances of such were the Trade Union Unity League (1930–34), the League of Struggle for Negro Rights (1934), the National Negro Congress (1935–39), the Southern National Negro Youth Congress, the International Labor Defense (1928–34), the Southern Conference on Human Welfare (1938), (not to be confused with the entirely legitimate and thoroughly anti-communist Southern Regional Council, of which two distinguished American prelates, Cardinal Stritch and Cardinal Spellman, have expressed their approval).

Characteristic of these communist agencies is the absence of any really constructive program and their eager exploiting of any flagrant instance of injustice which may further their cause, particularly where there is an opportunity to create great bitterness, resentment, and excitement. Their aim is rapidly to build up as vigorously as possible a crusading case to be advertised on an international scale and thereby obtain a public hearing. Thus they can raise funds and throw suspicion on any other group that has undertaken to try to seek justice in this same instance. Out of this they look to either of two contrary results: one is to induce others to join with them, for instance, by circulating petitions and inducing the usual quota of communist sympathizers, fellow-travelers, and pseudo-liberal innocents who go along with what they illusorily conceive as a genuinely liberal movement. By the same token the communists manage to frighten away the more cautious and discerning citizens and leave the field of championship of civil rights completely in their own hands. Their aim is to be first on the scene with the most adherents, the most noise, the most advertising and the most aggressive and abrasive tactics. At the same time, they show a sublime indifference to reaching any really definite conclusion for the case that they advocate. It is to their interest to prolong "celebrated cases" indefinitely and use them as an opportunity for spreading among the susceptible minority peoples at home or abroad the thesis that the communists alone are the saviors of the world.

Where, therefore, such agencies come into play, it is of great importance that we do not let ourselves be deceived. If one is asked to engage in projects like signing public manifestos or taking part in public meetings, it is well to insist that one should be in at the formation of such projects so as to know not only what are the original aims but who are the personalities involved. The subtlety of communist tactics is an added reason for frequent consultation with organizations that have a clear anti-communist record, such as those we have mentioned, in order to be able to spot the deceptive element where we have a certain suspicion that it exists.

Speaking at the Catholic Interracial Forum in New York City on February 16, 1956, Alvin Stokes, former Negro investigator for a congressional subcommittee on un-American activities, pointed out that at the time of his investigation, in 1949, the ratio of Negro communists to the total Negro population was that of one in 10,000, whereas the ratio in the white population, at the same period, was one in 1,000.

From the beginning of the disturbances in Alabama and elsewhere in the spring of 1956, it was plain that the American communists would seize, as they did, with eager glee upon the white resistance movements and any accompanying racial disorders. They saw in them a golden opportunity to exploit popular fears and resentments and inflame everyone and anyone to violent outbreaks. But the American Negroes, many of whose leaders had been deluded by the communist in the late twenties and early thirties, were now determined to close ranks and keep the party's invasion at bay.

On February 21, 1956, Frederick Woltman, a recognized authority on communists and communist machinations, wrote in the *New York World-Telegram and Sun:*

"The communist party is trying to crash the fight for civil rights in the South.

"And the country's largest Negro organization, which has been accused of working in league with communists by White Citizens Councils in the South, has taken steps to head off the Reds' move.

"Each of the 1,300 local branches and youth councils of the National Association for the Advancement of Colored People has received a stern warning that the communists are making 'intensive efforts' to infiltrate the nation-wide civil rights assembly in Washington, March 4–6.

"Roy Wilkins, NAACP executive secretary, directed his membership to exercise special care in selecting delegates, in order to avoid any possibility that the assembly would be "captured" by left-wing individuals and groups. Otherwise, Mr. Wilkins added, 'the whole civil rights movement will receive a black eye and we will get very little attention, if any, by the Congress.'

"About 2,000 delegates attended from fifty-one national organizations. Among them, besides the NAACP, were the Catholic Interracial Council, YWCA, National Council of Jewish Women, American Jewish Congress and American Jewish Committee, AFL-CIO, and various church groups.

"They're seeking legislation in this Congress against what the leaders call 'a breakdown in law and order in some parts of the South' where the Constitution and Supreme Court 'are being flouted openly.' The communist party in the *Daily Worker* last week officially called for support of 'the mass lobby.'

" 'You know,' the NAACP leader told its branches, 'that our national policy is not to co-operate with any communist-front or left-wing group. Of course, we do not work with communists.'

" 'In sending delegates to Washington,' said Mr. Wilkins, 'you are assuming responsibility for the good name of the NAACP.' No communist front is included in the fifty-one assembly sponsors, he pointed out.

"Since the recent violence in Alabama, the communist party has been aggressively exploiting the desegregation issue."

THE CITIZEN IN THE COMMUNITY

In general, the Catholic layman concerned with the minority problems from the standpoint of Christian teaching needs to be clear as to the role of the citizen in the community, the fact that he is a citizen of two worlds: religious and secular. In each of these and in both of these he has a duty and an opportunity.

This duty and this opportunity are particularly evident in cases where the individual can exert an influence in determining the policies of public institutions. The individual cannot be indifferent if human rights or civil rights are concerned, as in the case of school boards, welfare organizations, and hospitals.

As evidence that this difficulty is by no means insurmountable we need only remember the wonderful success with which courageous action was crowned in the case of the Mercy Hospital in Charleston, West Virginia. When three Negro girls were taken on as nurses in that institution the majority of the white nurses left in protest. Undismayed by this action, Mother Mary Catherine, the superintendent, quietly informed those who protested that they were discharged and then telephoned all over the United States for recruits to take their place. Positions were soon filled, and the three Negro nurses were completely assimilated. Particularly happy was the result that the hospital reported not only no objection on the part of the physicians or the trustees, but a closer and better relation between the trustees and the medical faculty as a result of this development. This was a case in which direct and courageous action worked, and worked well.

CATHOLIC HOSPITALS

Speaking in October, 1955, to the Committee on Hospitals of the Catholic Interracial Council of Chicago, Cardinal Stritch outlined at some length the genuinely Catholic position on this last-mentioned point, a position which is steadily gaining ground, and is already accepted in a large number of Catholic hospitals of the nation. His remarks strongly emphasized the following points:

(1) The *principles* are beyond dispute. The question is how to carry them out in practice. "If there is one thing clear in the Church's doctrine, it is that there can be no distinction of color, no distinction of race or nationality." St. Paul embodied that

146

principle in one of his Epistles (to the Romans) and the Apostles followed it in preaching the Gospel. It was clearly embodied in the life of the early Church, and was never contradicted.

(2) We in the United States have built up the greatest system of hospitals in the world. Even a private hospital "exists for a public purpose. It exists for a public charity, and . . . tax exemption is the equivalent of contribution, so that while they are private in the sense that they are not conducted with tax money they are not private in the sense that they are no concern of the public authorities and the civil authorities." Civil authority rightly exercises supervision of the standards of hospitals and the qualifications of those who minister in them.

(3) We need the fullest co-operation between staff and hospital. "Where there are distinctions in the admittance of qualified doctors into a staff there is something doing which is not in the public good, and certainly which is offensive to our Christian sense of what is right. . . . Where a staff refuses to admit a qualified man, because of color, that staff is not envisioning its responsibility in the community and certainly is not envisioning the principle upon which we are basing these discussions today."

(4) As for the sick, "how can we kneel before our blessed Saviour on the cross with His arms outstretched for all, and limit our charity and limit our ministration to any particular group?" The argument drawn from our need of pay patients is, with our progress, "getting less and less force. And courageous action will make that argument entirely ineffective and without weight . . . A hospital cannot do an unlimited work of charity . . . But in the doing of everything, it can look at man just as God looks at man, and without making distinctions of any sort."

COMMUNITY ACTION

It would be a mistake to confine our efforts simply to the removal of misconceptions. Important as such a work is, it is but the beginning, the necessary condition for the substantial task of building up a structure of racial unity and harmony. Our real aim is to obtain positive co-operation of all races and groups toward the common good.

Valuable and necessary as it is to approach the problem of prejudice directly through enlightenment and refutation, the most effective way to deal with it is to enlist the co-operation of different groups for a common interest in the good of the community. This applies particularly where neighborhood problems are concerned and can very often be most effectively put into effect by undertaking some specific, simple and clearly definable project, as in the field of public service, health facilities, local crime prevention, etc. It is not just a question of tolerating and patiently enduring the proximity of people who are culturally unsympathetic to us, but of enlisting new forces, new energies and enthusiasms, in order to create a better neighborhood. In the atmosphere of such community co-operation, antagonisms disappear of themselves. People come to know each other as persons in their own right. They become accustomed to regard each other as citizens filling different offices or bearing various responsibilities in the community. They are interested in the fact that they have different interests and talents. In that way they do not *primarily* look upon one another as members of this or that racial or national-origin group. And all are proud to be identified with the common interests that unite us all, as Americans, as citizens of their state, as contributors to the common welfare and defense, or, again, as members of the respective parish or church.

USING LOCAL RESOURCES

Recent experience in the field of organized community co-operation has emphasized the apparently unfailing resources of the American people for precisely this type of unified effort. The American capacity for constructive local co-operation is a phenomenon of American life which seems to impress visitors to our country. Sufficient experience has been gathered along this line to guide beginners in this field. One of its most effective forms is the mobilization of purely local resources in order to deal with local problems, problems which fail to yield to a purely administrative approach.

In other words, there are plenty of troublesome local disorders that can be cleaned up, or run-down areas that by a modicum of intelligent effort can be repaired and renewed. Improvements can be made in the outward face of dilapidated neighborhoods, or morale restored where it has broken down because of delinquency and civic neglect. In a large number of instances it is not necessary to call in the services of outside paid experts or the services of national or city-wide organizations. In so many cases the resources of the neighborhood itself are amply sufficient. The leadership is right there at home. The same talent for leadership that is applied so effectively to local political party organization is a sign of what can be mobilized for entirely non-political causes as well. It is latent among the local representatives of various fields such as labor, the professions, the clergy, education, industry, public welfare, police, municipal employment and both public and private welfare.*

* For an example of such action in practice see Appendix B.

Such a local organized community, in taking stock of its own needs, can profitably inquire into the situation of the local Negro community.

CITIZENS' COMMUNITY CHECKLIST

Chester Bowles has proposed a citizens' checklist for communities both north and south of the Mason-Dixon line. It might include, he says, the following questions:

How many Negroes are in the police force? The fire department? City Hall? The school system?

Do Negroes have a full opportunity to get such jobs? And if so, are they promoted solely on merit and services?

What kind of housing is available to Negroes—both public and private? What kind of medical and hospital care?

Is there any direct or indirect discrimination in public housing and entertainment facilities?

What about private enterprise jobs? Do Negro workers have jobs which use their skill to the fullest?

Is vocational, professional training freely available to Negroes?

Are the police and the courts as fair to them as to other sections of the population?

Each community might make a list of its strong and weak points and go to work to patch up the latter.

THE CHANGING PARISH

It is important that we have, first of all, a realistic understanding of how much leverage parochial opinion actually has in such situations. In practically all cities Catholics will be a minority in their neighborhoods. Yet, their opinion may be the dominant influence if it is concerted and well led. Whereas most other religious denominations dispose of properties in Negro areas and follow their congregations to the suburbs, Catholic churches and schools remain at old locations to serve new residents. This policy of permanence is an invaluable asset in reenforcing the sense of security needed in transition areas.

It frequently happens that Catholic Negro families when they move into white parishes are not warmly welcomed by their fellow Catholics—at church, in the schools, in parish society, and in the life of the parish. This attitude has been responsible for many Negro families leaving the Church.

Right Rev. John O'Grady, secretary of the National Conference of Catholic Charities, has remarked:

"When people in many of our parishes talk about conservation, they are talking about keeping out Negroes. This, we know, is a hopeless task today and it is utterly at variance with our Christian philosophy of life. We are dedicated to the universalism of Christian charity. We know that Christ's Redemption was intended for all people. . . . We are anxious to extend the hand of fellowship and brotherhood in Christ to all peoples. Now what does this mean in relation to our attitude toward the Negro in our cities? It means that we must extend the hand of fellowship and of brotherhood and love to him. It means that we must welcome him into our neighborhoods. His coming does not necessarily mean the deterioration of our neighborhoods and parishes. We can bring him into our organizations, into our conservation movement; we can have him join with us in maintaining good standards in our housing and in our neighborhood as a whole."

Two great centers in our country where the neighborhood problem is particularly acute offer instances of what practically can be done: Chicago and Philadelphia. As in all our great urban concentrations of recently migrated Negro populations, they are faced with the two ever-present problems: the black ghetto and the job ceiling, the problems of home and of employment.

About two years ago some 150 pastors of the archdiocese of Chicago were called together by Cardinal Stritch to discuss the place of the Church in neighborhood conservation in that city. At this meeting Cardinal Stritch pointed the way ahead for his priests and people. "There are," he said, "in our city certain areas that are called 'near-blight' areas. The experts have studied them and they have marked them out on the map . . . The realization that they can be saved has to be infused into these neighborhoods. Then, if the people of these areas work together under proper guidance, doing rather simple things, and if public authority enforces the law, blight in these areas can be prevented. . . . We are in a position to do a great deal toward building up neighborliness and self-help in our neighborhoods." He also emphasized another salient point: "Naturally, there is another phase to our pastoral problem. We can not only reclaim some of the blighted areas . . . but we can prevent other areas from becoming blighted."

PRESERVING THE NEIGHBORHOOD

"Flight from the old Chicago neighborhoods is not inevitable," Monsignor O'Grady has observed. "The experience of a number of pastors has already demonstrated that something can be done about it. Many of them have profited by the experience of the older parishes."

As for the "simple things" to which Cardinal Stritch referred, people can get together for the purpose of discussing ways and means of keeping their houses in good repair, and find means of mutual assistance. They can discover methods of making the neighborhood a proper place for the maintenance of family life. "These simple things," remarks Monsignor O'Grady, "do not require elaborate organization and yet they help people to grow up; they give them an appreciation of their own strength. As they gain strength, they will be ready to face new problems. They will want to discuss what can be done in an over-all program for housing in their district or neighborhood."

A writer in the *Louisville Courier-Journal* for May 23, 1954, thus describes the conservation movement in the "Back of the Yards" neighborhood in Chicago, in which the Catholic priests have joined together with other groups:

"Thousands of families in this once underprivileged and rundown area have teamed together to produce an amazing rejuvenation.

"Driven by a fierce pride in their homes, churches, families and old associations, they've abandoned the practice of 'letting George do it.'

"For the first time in a generation, new homes are being built on old vacant lots. There's the gleam of new white paint on once run-down houses. Local banks are beginning to increase the dollars available for home-improvement loans."

A DETAILED PLAN

Coming down more precisely to the question of the simple things to do, a couple of laymen, John McDermott and Dennis Clark, members of the Catholic Interracial Council of Philadelphia and both experienced in quelling interracial disputes, have worked out a plan for preventing hasty decisions in all-white neighborhoods when a family of a different race moves in.* "The abiding problem in the city is not violence," they say, "but the frigid withdrawal of whites from the presence of Negro neighbors. The white owners lose confidence in their homes and their neighborhoods, and sell as quickly as possible. There are no really rational reasons why this process takes place, for the mentalities behind it are dominated by fear, pride, exasperation and even hysteria."

For residents who feel that something "must be done" when their neighborhood property values seem to be threatened, the authors offer six suggestions:

(1) Stay put. Don't sell your house and run away to a heavier mortgage. You will probably have to sell at a loss if all the area properties are dumped on the market in a panic.

(2) Organize. Form a block or neighborhood group, open to *all* citizens and races.

(3) See your realty dealers and ask them to assist in keeping the area stable. Make clear that families of all races who are good neighbors in the civic sense of the term are welcome. Point out that in view of present trends, no 'exclusive' wall can be built around any area.

(4) Squelch rumors. Try to calm excited talk and dispel any untrue or half-true statements about the neighborhood or racial matters in general.

(5) Guard the neighborhood's housing standards. Have your group or civic organization watch closely all zoning changes, conversions, overcrowding or signs of dilapidation. Housing regulations should be well known and city officials should be promptly notified if services begin declining.

* *Interracial Review*, August, 1955.

INTERRACIAL EVENTS

Much can be accomplished in the way of interracial harmony through carefully prepared and impressive events. In the preparation of these events and their sponsorship ample opportunity is provided for precisely that type of interracial co-operation which, as we have seen, is one of the basic key policies of the Catholic interracial movement. Such events can be of a religious character, such as special church services, special devotions, Communion breakfasts, forums, speakers, essay contests. It would be wearisome to go into detail. Suggestions on this point can be easily obtained from any of the Catholic Interracial Councils. Several great fundamental results are achieved by such carefully planned events. First of all, by their very nature, they are of an educational character in the way in which they are planned and carried out. They illustrate the concept of fraternal unity and the catholicity of the Church. Again, they offer an excellent opportunity for competent speakers to address the audience. Where the events are not of a strictly religious character, the Catholic audience can learn some of the garnered wisdom of intelligent and God-fearing men and women outside the Church, many of whom have borne the heat and burden of the day. At the same time a hospitable occasion offers the opportunity to many people not of our Faith to learn much of the Church's attitude and thereby to join with us more willingly in work for the common good.

Such events are, as one might say, a measure of growth. From year to year they offer us an opportunity to take stock and see how we have progressed.

A WORD FROM THE PULPIT

A growing number of Catholic bishops and priests have become convinced of the good that can be accomplished by a periodical, practical sermon outlining the Church's dogma and guidance on interracial justice. Such a sermon, carefully prepared, delivered on a high level of wisdom and understanding and sanctioned by the ordinary of the diocese can do an immense amount of good. Preaching is especially necessary in view of the frequent complaint of the Catholic faithful that they never heard of this topic from the pulpit. No matter how persuasive are one's arguments in private, they are not infrequently met with the objection that we have never heard this subject preached. Yet the opportunities are great. In the course of a year's sermon scheme there is always room for one specifically prepared discourse, let us say, on the Kingdom of Christ, the racial unity of the Church, the interpretation of papal encyclicals, such as would be a necessary part of the instruction of our Catholic people. In the explanation of the Epistles and Gospels a thoughtful preacher can find numberless telling instances to enforce the lessons of justice and charity.

COMMUNING IN CHRIST

Once more let it be emphasized that we are here dealing with the integrity of living human beings, our brethren in this earthly lot, and our brethren in our holy faith as persons dear to God and sharing our destiny. The city, the school, the labor organization, the state, society itself—are all but expressions of the human individual as he appears in the different aspects of his earthly career. Hence the primary importance of maintaining throughout a profoundly spiritual approach to all problems of human relations. Nowhere is that better illustrated, as I have already said, than in the Mass itself, its meaning and its participation; a type of knowledge which is not as widely diffused as it might be.

We need again to recall that the Mass *is* the sacrifice of reconciliation between all races and peoples: "our Peace," in the words of the Apostle St. Paul. Through the Eucharistic sacrifice, the sacrifice of the cross is brought to us in space and time. The very act of breaking down human differences, of uniting them in the higher unity of the children of God is re-enacted each day upon our altars. It is not just a proclamation of peace, it is not just a motion or gesture, so to speak, in favor of peace, but it is the enactment of human unity in the Person of the God Man, the Redeemer and the Head of the human race.

The faithful, as Pope Pius XII so carefully points out in his encyclical *Mediator Dei* on the holy liturgy, when they attend Mass and unite themselves with the ceremony do so not just as individuals united with their God but as a community. The sacrifice of the Holy Eucharist is a sacrifice offered for the community by the priest as representative of the Church, but in their own way, according to their own condition by all who take part. It is a community act in which we worship as one family. By the very act of sharing in this holy sacrifice we both create and assert our mystical oneness.

When we receive Holy Communion this unity of the religious community is reinforced. We are made one in a mysterious and most marvelous fashion through our unity not only with the divinity of Christ but with His Body and Blood as well. And this is particularly significant in connection with the question of racial differences. Since these differences rest upon bodily characteristics, since we carry the source of contention in our body, there is a peculiar fitness that this bodily differentiation should be transcended and overcome through our union with the sacred Body of Jesus Christ. The distinctions of body and blood among men are transcended by unity with the Body and Blood of Christ.

Epilogue

Let us say a few words in conclusion about moderation, about following a course that avoids extremes.

The events that centered around the University of Alabama, in the first months of 1956, made talk of moderation very popular. People around the country and in the deep South itself were shocked by the language and threats of the white extremists. Aggressive die-hards made tremendous emotional appeal and posed as defenders of liberty and the sanctity of white womanhood. A co-ed at the University of Alabama reported that she had wept the whole night through because a Negro girl (Autherine Lucy)—about whom the excitement turned— had been admitted to the campus. Old resentments were stirred up, and the White Citizens Councils, established in order to combat desegregation and defend white supremacy, began to talk in old Ku Klux Klan overtones.

Many people in the South, however, who entertained no deep-seated prejudices became seriously alarmed at reports of extremism on the part of the Negro leaders and of communist influence. Some papers in Washington, D.C., and vicinity began to publish a series of allegations against the already integrated schools: stories of improper conduct on the part of the Negro children, of juvenile crime. These stories were not documented, they originated from anonymous sources, but fears are easily played upon when they fit into a preconceived pattern. It is easier to scare people by telling them things are all wrong in a school than to reassure them through accurate information that things are going quite according to normal.

Popular resentment again was aroused by the charge that the Supreme Court was favoring the use of force, in spite of the Court's temperate and carefully guarded language. Those who advocated the use of legal measures in the defense of the Negro's civil rights—and only legal measures—were credited with demanding the use of Federal bayonets upon a terror-stricken white South. Talk of violence readily leads to violence; and where imaginations are excited, individuals will say and do things of which they would not dream in more normal times.

For a balanced view of the situation, it is important, therefore, to keep the following several points in mind.

(1) The Negro leaders of the country, North and South alike, despite their intense emotion over the bitter resistance to the Supreme Court's decree, were surprisingly calm and moderate in their pronouncements. Immediately after the May 17, 1954, decree the tone was set by Dr. Channing H. Tobias, chairman of the board of the National Association for the Advancement of Colored People. In an address at Atlanta, Dr. Tobias committed himself and his organization to a policy of moderate, patient cultivation of understanding and the use of purely legal methods. The same tone was maintained throughout, and the Negroes, with few exceptions, were determined to meet hate and bitterness not in kind, but with the weapon of reason, patience, and love.

Characteristic were the words spoken in Montgomery, Alabama, on February 23, 1956, by a Baptist minister, Rev. Martin Luther King, Jr., head of the Montgomery Improvement Association, which directed the continuing boycott organized by

Negroes on December 5, as a protest against the arrest of a
Negro woman, Rosa Parks, who had refused to give up a seat
in the white section of the bus. Dr. King informed the gathering that the protest was not against a single incident, but over
things that "go deep down into the archives of history."

"We have known humiliation, we have known abusive language, we have been plunged into the abyss of oppression," he
told them, "and we decided to rise up only with the weapon
of protest. It is one of the greatest glories of America that we
have the right of protest."

"There are those who would try to make of this a hate cam-
paign," the Atlanta-born, Boston-educated Baptist minister
said. "This is not war between the white and the Negro, but
a conflict between justice and injustice. This is bigger than the
Negro race revolting against the white. We are seeking to improve not the Negro of Montgomery but the whole of Montgomery.

"If we are arrested every day, if we are exploited every day,
if we are trampled over every day, don't ever let anyone pull
you so low as to hate them. We must use the weapon of love.
We must have compassion and understanding for those who
hate us. We must realize so many people are taught to hate us
that they are not totally responsible for their hate. But we stand
in life at midnight, we are always on the threshold of a new
dawn."*

MEANING OF MODERATION

Let us ask ourselves, then: Just where does a moderate really
stand? The word itself can be abused, like all good and useful
expressions. It can be used as an excuse for simply doing noth-

* *New York Times,* February 24, 1956, p. 8.

ing, for contenting oneself with purely verbal pronouncements, for adroitly avoiding a very real issue under the guise of discretion. Where talk is superfluous, you act "moderately" when you wisely say nothing. But when the public expects the individual to stand up and be counted, where the honor of our country or our holy faith is at stake, then a policy of silence is no longer a true policy of moderation; it can readily skirt the edge of cowardice.

The real moderate, as I see him, is one who has made a definite choice, hard or painful as that may be. He is one who recognizes the many steps that ordinarily are needed in order to attain a given end. In the question of race relations, he (or she) is alive to the need of creating a favorable climate of opinion, by the intelligent use of ordinary and of mass media. The moderate person is deeply convinced of the need of personal integrity and consistency. Those of us, for instance, in the North can be charged with inconsistency who are content to point our fingers at the South and forget, as Senator John F. Kennedy of Massachusetts has remarked, that the worst outbreaks of racial violence in recent years have been not in the South, but in several of our large northern urban centers.

GRADUALISM

The Latin word for steps or degrees is *gradus,* which brings into focus the much-discussed term gradualism.

If by a gradual approach you mean taking steps so slow and uncertain as to arrive at no tangible result, the term will greatly please those persons who do not wish to have anything done, and are thankful for some verbal excuse for neglecting it. The word, by the same token, will be equally objectionable to persons who look for results and are weary of much talk and scant action.

A policy of moderation is a strong policy, when it is sincere; it is sincere when its caution or deliberateness is directed toward genuine progress. In the last analysis, the question is not of speed or of delay so much as that of making a real beginning, be it ever so slight, here and now. We cannot make too frequent and earnest a plea for moderation, patience, tolerance, and mutual good will. And it is certainly true, as is frequently said, that "extremism will get us nowhere." On the other hand, a pious dilettantism can keep us indefinitely on dead center.

When the president of Spring Hill College, Alabama, Rev. Andrew J. Smith, S.J., was recently asked how the college had managed in the admission of Negro students, he replied it had acted without publicity or fanfare. In his own words, "We simply performed a quiet surgical operation on current prejudices by admitting Negroes." Once the operation was performed, things took a normal course. The students were absorbed without incident or commotion into the life of the college.

Many thousands of such quiet surgical operations are being performed over the entire country. The operation succeeded at Spring Hill because the members of the college community already had learned, in the course of their Catholic education, something of the Church's teaching on the matter of race relations and the treatment of one's neighbor. But operations cannot be performed without some preparations. The more thoroughly the "climate of opinion" is prepared by intelligent teaching in our institutions and parishes, or by wide publicity in our communities, the less disturbance will such "operations," such incidents, create; the sooner will wounds to pride or selfishness be healed.

Christ our Lord, in order to prove and to maintain His claim as the Son of the living God, was obliged to probe deeply the sensitiveness and collective pride of His fellow countrymen. Yet He acted "gradually," that is to say, He prepared their minds by His teaching and His divine example: as by His thirty years at Nazareth, by the Sermon on the Mount, and by the profound pedagogy of His miracles.

Those who wish to prove that our fellow man is truly human, and should enjoy the dignity and rights of a human being, must also prepare the way, and, as I have said frequently before, it is a work in which all concerned must join.

At the turning point of his Spiritual Exercises, that great master of the spiritual life, St. Ignatius Loyola, asks his retreatant to consider the example of several types of men. Some deliberate about correcting their lives; entertain fine sentiments, but go no further. Others attempt a compromise, try to carry water on both shoulders and please both God and the devil. The third type, those whom he recognizes as genuine and sincere, bravely choose the means that lead to the end, the sacrifices necessary for the wholehearted service of their Creator and Lord.

Ignatius hurries no one; gives you days, months, if you so wish, to deliberate. But he means action in the end. No matter how long delayed, the decisions must be made. We must recognize that certain roads lead nowhere; they are dead ends and blind alleys. Such a dead end, such a blind alley, is the path of racial segregation. Despite all fine talk and attempts to idealizing, despite any use or justification it had or may have had in earlier times and under earlier conditions, today it leads but into a cul-de-sac. Its pursuit breeds disorders infinitely greater than any evils which it seeks to avoid.

To avoid a dead end, to refuse to switch into a blind alley, does not mean we have reached our journey's goal. To have performed the surgical operation and to have renounced racial segregation as a policy by no means certifies that we have settled the problem of race relations. A long journey, up hill, down dale, across many a river and swamp, may be stretched ahead before we have reached the promised land where, in Pope Pius XII's words, we can live together in order and in tranquility. Nor can this book carry you there. I shall be satisfied if it but accomplishes two things:

(1) help guide the American public out of what at best is a hopeless impasse;

(2) indicate a few of the many practical and useful ways in which we can travel forward together toward the peace and unity of Jesus Christ.

The road of constructive race relations, like many other rough roads, leads upward and outward. It frees us from the vicious circle of an ever-recurrent contradiction and opens for us the wider field of our relations, as Americans, with the people of the entire world. It gives us an infinitely precious clue to a lasting and fruitful foreign policy and to a membership in the fellowship of nations. Such an acquisition is thoroughly honorable for our own national ideas as well as welcome to the other peoples of the world.

We do not solve the race-relations problem of our own township or city district for ourselves alone; we are contributing to the strength and dynamism of the entire nation. In the same way, what we do here in this country contributes to the strength and dynamism of the entire free world. If we have derived our principles and our standards from God as the common Father and the end and destiny of us all, our achievements will be strong with the strength of His wisdom and grace. We will speak with strength and conviction to the millions still blind to His truth, to those who are deaf to the appeal of His holy name. And as Catholics our full, frank, and unequivocal recognition of the equal worth and dignity of all men will indicate that profound source from which our holy faith derives its eternal and youthful freshness, its ever-driving, conquering power: in union with the Christ who died and rose for all.

Now that I have reached the end of my discussion, I think of many paths I would have liked the reader to explore.

I should like to have discussed the qualifications of those who mean to take an active part in working for better race relations. It would be worth while to draw up the specifications of the real interracial apostle.

In many ways this would be like drawing plans for a building. This is why, I imagine, St. Paul talked in many dimensions when he spoke of the charity of Christ: its length, its breadth, its depth, and its height.

The *length:* It is not only what you do just now but what you do over a space of time; the time tests your effort. The effect is seen in not just the result of the immediate action but the cumulative result of the years.

The *breadth:* You succeed only when your work rests upon the broad basis of our common interest, not on that of a single group or class. Racism applied in one direction always breeds racism in reverse, which may be precisely what we shall have to face in future decades in a largely non-white world.

The *depth:* We have to examine the details and register the realities. You may have turned aside and from the blind alley, but there is still tough jungle to hack through in the long battle against crime, illiteracy and social retardation with their corresponding psychic disorders.

Finally, the *height:* The need of keeping our sights raised to Him who is the Source of grace, of light, and of strength, the Source of the grace that is needed to bring order out of confusion. St. Paul uses the word edification, *aedificare,* to construct a house, an *aedes.* It is an architectonic idea. While we are working for our fellow man, we are at the same time building a temple to Almighty God; we are constructing the Mystical

Body in this world and we are building up the Christ personality in the individual.

THE AMERICAN INDIAN

I should like to have said something about some of the other racial questions in the United States, though in these I have much less personal experience; about the American Indian, for instance.

It would be worth while to draw up in perspective and note the correspondences as well as differences in situation between the Indian and the Negro. When the Indian is removed from his reservation, he is relocated—to use the technical Government expression, about which the Department of the Interior has very much to say. When he is relocated, let us say, in Los Angeles or San Francisco or Minneapolis, he meets with difficulties of housing, of neighborhood tensions, consequences like those that face the Negro. Segregation in the case of the Indian is not as overt. We have no formal policy on a wide scale of segregating Indians; nevertheless, the phenomenon is frequent and there are lots of real discriminations, often of a very painful character. These are all the more galling because the Indian is the aboriginal citizen of this country and retains, in most cases, his early national consciousness.

On the other hand, the lot of the tribal Indian is very different from that of the Negro. Conditions vary so radically between the different tribes that any general pronouncement would be misleading. Some Indians have completely evolved out of all need or relationship to tribal lands, tribal institutions. They are ready and glad to take their full part in the mainstream of the nation's life. Some of these, in fact, do not suffer any particular discrimination but have completely acclimated themselves. The Iroquois Indians, for instance, from the Caughnawaga Reservation, near Montreal, make an excellent living, working as specialized construction workers in Brooklyn.

At the opposite end of the Indian spectrum there are highly self-contained tribes, like the Zuñis and the Hopis and other tribes of the American Southwest, who are enclosed in a highly intricate complex of tribal usages, language, ceremonial, and local political self-government, and jealously resent any interference from outside. Their tribes are traditionally of keen interest to the anthropologist, and present special problems to the missionary. Again, other Indian tribes, like the Navahos, are still painfully aware of their lack of education, of health facilities, and their dire need for retaining their share of the tribal land. They are still dependent on the aid of the Federal Government, on Federal educational and social institutions.

The casual observer of Indian affairs is quite bewildered by the many-sided conflict of influences and agencies that it involves, such as (1) various types of greedy speculators, ranging from land sharks to highly public-minded but predatory corporations, who are eager to lay their hands upon the Indian's lands; (2) the Government itself and its various agencies, subject of high praise in some respects and considerable criticism in others; (3) various state governments which fluctuate in their interest between the Indian and interest in the various political and economic agencies concerned; (4) the organized voice of the Indians themselves, united in the American Indian Congress, as a means of publicity; (5) the organized friends of the Indians, such as the Association on American Indian Affairs, with headquarters in New York City, and (6) last, but not least, the missions, with their men and women dedicated, often under great hardship and poverty, to bringing the Christian Gospel to the Indians and alleviating their sufferings.

Add to all this the complexities that result from the Indians themselves, with their great variety of languages, all of them extremely recondite and difficult not only for the white man but for each other. Nevertheless, in spite of all these handicaps, the American Indian, far from vanishing, is increasing steadily in number. Individual tribes may pass out of existence, but the American Indian as a whole is developing, advancing, and multiplying.

SPANISH-AMERICANS

In connection with the Catholic viewpoint on race relations, there is certainly a vast amount to say on the question of the Spanish-American population in the United States if we regard them, as we can only partially do, from a racial standpoint. These fall roughly into three main divisions. (1) There are the original Spanish-Americans of our Southwest, such as the Hispanos of New Mexico and Arizona. (2) The very large Mexican-American population is composed, for the most part, of workers on our railroads and in our mines and on our farms, who cross the border legally and illegally and are spread from the Rio Grande far north and east up to the Great Lakes and the Canadian border itself. (3) Finally, Puerto Ricans are recent arrivals, for the most part, in our Northeastern cities. They are distinguished from other Spanish-Americans in being the first people to come to the mainland of this country from a mission territory, as well as being the first large Spanish-speaking immigration to the Northeastern United States.

Here we are dealing with the question not so much of race as of conflicting cultures, the problem of assimilation—and of a religious point of view. It is only recently that we as Catholics have really begun to realize on a large scale and in an as yet only partly organized fashion the magnitude of the religious challenge.

Many-sided as are the needs of our Spanish-American neighbors, let us bear in mind that the ideas that we have proposed at some length in this book of aiding Negro-white relations in our urban and suburban neighborhoods apply also in a practical fashion to relations of the Spanish-speaking people with regard to the rest of the local community. In other words, if Negroes and whites can learn to live together in peace and order, so can the other elements in our neighborhoods learn to be adjusted as well. The same vicious circles are created through injustice. The same wide fields exist, of general human problems of retardation, of backwardness, of unpreparedness for civic life. In the latter area, particularly, an immense amount of work toward developing citizenship is to be done with the Spanish-Americans in excess of what is needed for the Negroes. The Negroes, for the most part, have long traditions in this country and have developed a fair degree of political consciousness and party organization. Many Spanish-Americans, however, are quite new to our ways. Very elementary ideas as to their part in the civic community have to be explained to them from the ground up.

In any case, the same principle applies in all instances, that we have a common interest and a common stake in our faith, in our nation, and in the common determination to build unity out of a troublesome but a glorious diversity.

APPENDIX A

Interracial Marriage*

Interracial marriage, as its infrequency of occurrence in the United States of America indicates, is not a significant phase of American life. It seems true that minority racial groups are as uninterested in fostering interracial marriages as is the majority white group. It is also true that there is no important influence at work positively advocating the mixture of races by marriage. The question may be asked: Why, then, is so much attention paid to it?

Marriage is, without doubt, the most intimate social relationship experienced by man. It has become a symbol of group solidarity; the stronghold to be guarded at any price. Thus, in one sense, interracial marriage with its associated problems *is* the race problem. In fact, marriage generally implies a social equality of parties. When interracial marriage is permitted, a certain basic equality is admitted, but not all are ready to admit this basic equality when other races are involved.

The avenues leading to a sane and sound evaluation of the problems presented by interracial marriage have been blocked in part by the aberrations of racism: the theory that one ethnic

* *Interracial Review,* February, 1943; a condensation of an article in *The Priest,* by Very Rev. Joseph F. Doherty, Chancellor of the Diocese of Camden, New Jersey.

group is condemned by the laws of nature to hereditary inferiority and another group is marked off as hereditarily superior. Its corollary maintains that the hope of civilization is in keeping one race pure and eliminating the so-called inferior group, or keeping it segregated. The term "race" is used as the classification of large groups of mankind based on traits which are hereditary.

Free from all sympathy with racists, Holy Mother Church, to paraphrase the words of Pope Pius XII, proclaims to all her sons, scattered over the world, that the spirit, the teaching, and the work of the Church can never be other than that which St. Paul preached: "putting on the new [man], him who is renewed unto knowledge, according to the image of Him that created him. There is neither Gentile nor Jew, circumcision nor uncircumcision, barbarian nor Scythian, bond nor free. But Christ is all and in all" (Col. 3: 10-11).

Surely, an organization cannot make such claims in the muddled world of today and then, ostrich-like, bury its head in the sands of indifference and hear no evil. The Church has never done so. Time and again she has insisted on the essential worth of man. The condemnation of racism by Pope Pius XI is only one of such insistences. Social legislation, therefore, which smacks of a condemned racist doctrine—namely, preservation of "purity of race"—is at a tremendous disadvantage in proving its claim to being just a law. The Catholic Church is entirely out of sympathy with such legislation. No reasonable justification can be claimed for the deprivation, merely on the basis of difference of race, of the fundamental right to marry according to one's own choice.

Despite the fact that laws forbidding interracial marriage are in force in twenty-nine states of the United States, one will look long and hard to find sufficient reason to justify them on any basis that is not questionable.

The Roman Catholic Church, on the other hand, in no wise forbids interracial marriage as such. The Apostolic See alone can establish impediments to marriage for the baptized. The Apostolic See alone authentically interprets the divine law in so far as it establishes impediments to marriage. The universal Church, however, places no obstacle to interracial marriage. It may not be argued that since this has been mainly a local problem it would be left to the local Church authorities to legislate upon it.

On the contrary, it must be denied that the Apostolic See or the local ordinaries would be indifferent to moral problems in any given locality. If one will consult the acts and decrees of the Plenary Councils of Baltimore, the First Plenary Council of Latin America, the first four Provincial Councils of Quito, or the Archdiocesan Synod of Santiago, Cuba, of 1680, no law will be found forbidding such marriages. These councils and synods are mentioned because they represent localities where the mixture of races has and does exist on a large scale.

Interracial marriage may also be considered in the light of the right to marry according to one's own choice. The right to marry the person of one's choice means that there should be freedom to marry this particular person of one's own choice regardless of race, and, it is understood, to have children by this particular person. Its importance as a natural human right, therefore, is not to be underestimated.

There are, of course, certain obvious limits to this freedom of choice. Reason imposes many limits as well as the positive divine law. Neither the natural law nor divine positive law sets up any impediment to marriage based on mere difference of race.

Morally considered, entrance upon an interracial marriage is in itself a good act. *In general,* to enter upon marriage is in itself a morally good act. Difference of color or race may be present in a particular marriage. This difference, is, however, no more than an accidental concomitant. Hence, it does not change the primary moral goodness of entering upon marriage. It has been intimated above that the present writer is convinced that the laws of the various states in the United States which forbid interracial marriages are unjust. This conviction is based upon several considerations.

First, there is no equitable proportion between the good effect that may be claimed for these laws and the resulting loss of benefits to the individual and to society, stemming from the deprivation of the fundamental human right to marry the person of one's own choice. One such benefit is sacramental grace in the case of baptized persons.

Second, if the desired effect of the laws is the advantage of any one particular group (for example, the white group), this advantage is not for the common good. Such laws have not succeeded in attaining their avowed purpose, that is, to prevent the mixture of races, but have encouraged concubinage, deprived many persons of the opportunity to enjoy the legal and property rights which would follow from a legitimate marriage if they had been allowed to form it, and have perpetuated interracial conflict.

One reputable scientist, Dr. Melville J. Herskovits, claimed that about 70 per cent of Negroes manifest mixture with whites. The great number of mulattoes in this country is evidence of liaison. Although many liaisons were perfectly lawful, legitimate marriage is not possible in the majority of states. This argues concubinage of some sort. The laws have perpetuated interracial conflict because they have implicitly denied that that social equality exists which is the basis of marriage and all other social intercourse.

To base these laws on difference of race alone is contrary

to Christian teaching on such matters. Christianity preaches the essential equality of all men. These laws forbid without a just and proportionate reason one form of social intercourse that is a manifestation of this essential equality of all men regardless of race.

The Holy Roman Catholic Church has never prohibited her subjects from entering upon such marriages. Where such prohibitions have existed, she has deplored them and maintained that mere difference of race alone cannot justly form the basis of such a general prohibition.

At least one state has invalidated such a law. On October 28, 1948, the California Supreme Court denied the petition for rehearing of the respondent in Perez *vs.* Lippold (32 Advance California Report 757). The majority held sections 60 and 69 of the California Civil Code prohibiting marriages between white persons and members of certain racial groups invalid, as violative of the equal protection clause of the Federal Constitution and as being too vague and uncertain to constitute a valid regulation. The petitioners in this case were both Catholics and contended that the laws interfered with the practice of their religion.

The court, although divided 4 to 3, held the following principles: The right to marry is the right of individuals, not of racial groups; the essence of the right to marry is freedom to join in marriage with the person of one's own choice; a segregation statute for marriage necessarily impairs the right to marry.

In short, there is little to uphold the validity of the laws against interracial marriage. However, this is not to say that in every instance this type of marriage should be encouraged. It is true that the Church, ever a loving Mother, customarily discourages her children from contracting marriages which may involve disadvantage to the offspring, and to this end is disposed to support, within the limits of the divine law, the disposition of the civil authorities which tend toward the attainment of this worthy purpose. There are many moral and social reasons for such an attitude. But the Church suggests, admonishes, persuades; she does not impose or forbid.

The Manhasset Project*

Four years ago a small group of local citizens, men and women, met in the home of Mrs. Dorothy Fremont Grant, author and lecturer, at Manhasset, on Long Island. They wished to see what could be done to relieve the forlorn plight of the whites and Negroes living in the section of Manhasset Township known as "the Valley." They brought to this meeting no experience in slum clearance. They could develop no definite plan. Yet on January 12, 1949, the contract was signed for a two-million dollar housing project for the Manhasset Valley and the adjacent Port Washington areas, and construction will start this spring.

A few aspects of this achievement, which you will admit is a fair-sized one, deserve more than a passing notice. The story of the Manhasset Project shows that people *can* do something to help their neighbors out of what seems hopeless distress. It also indicates as to *how* this help can be given.

The neighbors who met at Mrs. Grant's house that January afternoon in 1945 were of different races and different faiths. There were four men and eight women: two of the women were colored and two were Jewish. It was a typical cross-

* John La Farge, S.J., in *Interracial Review*, June, 1949.

section of the Manhasset community. The blighted spot they were considering would have been bad enough if found in a backward country region, or even in the slums of a big city. It was particularly noticeable because the Valley families lived close to one of the wealthiest residential suburbs in the United States. Negroes and whites were found in Manhasset Valley, the Negroes occupying the dilapidated section. Heads of the families—fathers and mothers—were not unemployed. They had good paying jobs, most of them as domestics and gardeners in the nearby estates.

It was not a so-called "trouble area." The people who resided there set an example of decency and good Christian living that could make their more fortunate fellow citizens blush. Those familiar with the lives of these Valley citizens knew many an instance of their mutual kindliness and helpfulness. The Polish housewife, after her own day's job was done, visited her Negro neighbor whose wife was sick, washed the children, and cooked the meals for the family; just as the Negro housewife had done for the Polish friend a few weeks before.

The Negroes in the Valley were not complaining of discrimination, although, like Negroes pretty generally everywhere in the United States, they found it more difficult than white people to move out of a blighted neighborhood. Colored mothers in the Valley did not need to worry about what might happen to their children at school, since they were made welcome both in the public and the parish schools of the district. In fact, they were not *complaining* of anything, nor yet were they resigned and "accepting the situation." Cheerfully and bravely, along with their white neighbors, they were doing what little they could to try to improve their lot. But they were completely baffled by the sheer weight of stark physical misery, something that struck to the root of their home lives and warred against every effort to bring up their families as good Christians and citizens.

From the outset the initial committee determined two things, simple enough to mention yet easy enough to forget. They soon decided that some sort of housing project was imperatively needed, and that group action, not merely individual action, fortified by careful study, was required to put the project through.

Much can be done by the action of individuals—anybody, anywhere—who will proclaim whatever they may possess of the truth, and set a good personal example. For specific social projects, however, a solid groundwork of knowledge needs to be laid, unless more harm than good is to result. The efforts of even the most gifted and influential person are apt to be stultified if he trusts to himself alone and does not learn the difficult lesson of taking careful counsel and working with others.

The committee's first step, therefore, was to invite George K. Hunton, executive secretary of the Catholic Interracial Council of New York, to assist them in discussing the interracial question and the way a local community might deal with it. The plan that Mr. Hunton developed was not wholly new. Under the auspices of the New York City Board of Education, with certain public high schools as a center, it was already being tried out in several localities of New York City, as it had been in the "Back of the Yards" district of Chicago. From a parish angle, but still as a community project, it was promoted in the Rockaway Beach section of Queens County by Monsignor John J. Reddy, director of Catholic charities in the diocese of Brooklyn.

As formulated by the Catholic Interracial Council, the plan called for organized action by a typical cross-section of the local community—business and professional men, housewives, teachers and school principals, clergy, union officials, and social workers. This cross-section group took the lead in sponsoring a definite project for the community's good, and set up a community council to launch it. While they steered clear of any dependence upon the local politicians, the community council availed themselves of some of the practical methods used in the local organization of political parties. The sponsors employed every means to encourage all persons in the local community to work together, and to enlist in behalf of the project all available agencies, keeping, however, the enterprise strictly that of a local group working for local needs.

The original committee's studies soon led to an ambitious determination: to sponsor a first-class state housing project for the Valley and Port Washington. With the cordial endorsement of the local clergy, Catholic, Protestant and Jewish, the sponsors approached school teachers and various social agencies, and soon provided the community council with representatives from twenty sections of the Manhasset area.

The question of the real-estate brokers then arose. Obviously, they were not in a position to undertake the elaborate plan themselves. What would be their reaction to a state housing project planted in their neighborhood? At this point the planners learned another valuable lesson, which is that when you are trying to do the right thing and a genuinely unselfish thing, you can count upon much more good will than is usually anticipated. The real-estate men responded with enthusiasm, and lent their support, in turn, to the plan for the state project.

Another hurdle had to be cleared. Manhasset was unincorporated. To fill this legal vacuum the town board successfully petitioned the New York State Legislature to create a Town Housing Authority. The T.H.A.'s survey of the blighted districts, which was approved in January, 1947. Carried out according to standards prescribed by the New York State Housing

Commission, the survey proved conclusively the need of such action as the original committee had had in mind.

The survey disclosed that out of 191 living units in the Manhasset Valley section, housing some 700 Negroes, eighty-one needed major repairs. One-tenth of the Negro homes lacked electricity, water, heat or inside toilets; some lacked outside sewage; most of the houses were fire hazards. Overcrowding prevailed, to the extent of six or seven persons in three or four rooms. Thirty-one homes were simply unfit for human habitation. Some were merely garages or chicken coops. One was a store, with curtains as partitions.

On October 14, 1948, a loan of $2,000,000 was approved by the New York State Housing Commission for seventy home units in Port Washington at a cost of $802,755, and 100 units in the Manhasset Valley area at a cost of $1,197,245. Two other adjacent communities, Great Neck and Roslyn, also benefited by the project. Complete clearance for the work came in January of this year. To crown the enterprise a tract of twenty acres was acquired next to the Valley from John Hay Whitney, wealthy Manhasset resident, to be used as a state park. The project is self-financing, not a charity, and is only a nominal burden upon the local taxpayers. Rent for the apartments is pegged at $8.77 a room. The people living in the shacks were already paying good rentals.

The whites and Negroes in the Valley and vicinity have been living peaceably side by side—as they lived peaceably in the "mixed" areas of Detroit when some years ago the segregated areas of that city were swept by race riots. So they will continue to live together in friendship.

This was not a work done by charitable white people on behalf of Negroes, nor by charitable wealthy persons on behalf of the poor. The project was put through by *all* the members of a given community on behalf of all, without exception of race, color, creed or economic status. It was the total community mobilized, as a natural entity, to provide for its own needs. To do this, it made use of its own potential leadership. The difficulties the citizens of Manhasset experienced do not differ substantially from those that may occur in any other part of the United States or Canada. The plan they adopted, the steps they took, can be used in most communities.

Nobody but a fatuous humanitarian believes that families will be made good or pure or holy merely by good housing. But any woman can tell you that any other woman, of whatever condition or race she may be, can only with rare heroism succeed in raising and caring for her family when they are living in destitution in the midst of our expensive modern civilization. The women who joined with and inspired the men in the Manhasset Project were not wealthy philanthropists. They were mostly housewives or teachers who had no difficulty in seeing what it meant for any woman to work all day as a domestic and come back in the evening to homes of which one-third were without gas ovens for cooking and five per cent without any cooking facilities at all.

Certainly welfare projects may be distorted, and there are fanatics and subversives who make a business of distorting them and using human misery as a means to further their selfish economic and political ends. The best a housing project can do is to make it possible, or vastly easier, for people to lead good family lives. The inn to which the Good Samaritan carried his wounded acquaintance was only an inn—a mere convenience, not a means of sanctification. Our Saviour, however, immortalized the Samaritan's prudent action as an example of that sublimest of things, the perfect love of God and man.

By removing the conditions which breed race hatred, family decay and juvenile crime, we can open the way for the healing action of Him who alone can enter the human heart with His grace and make it whole. Modern times demand, it is true, modern methods of initiative, study, planning or organization and co-operation. Surely, the least the Saviour can ask of His followers is that we all use such means as are at our daily disposal in order to make it easier for people like ourselves to serve Him.

*   *   *

How did this all work out? Rawson Wood, president of Arwood Precision Casting Corporation of Brooklyn, a director of the Catholic Interracial Council and one of the members of the original group in Mrs. Grant's living room, has been a member of the North Hempstead Housing Authority since its formation, and became later its chairman. His experience taught him several valuable lessons in community organization. In his own words: "No matter what the controversy, it is unwise to assume that anyone is against you or that it is hopeless to convince him. Most people will do the right thing if given the chance to back down gracefully without loss of face, and the opportunity to participate without being pressured into it. Synthetic emotion aroused against you by pressure and money can usually be resisted by patience and courage."

Both developments—Spinney Hill Homes in Manhasset and Harbor Hill Homes in Port Washington—were completed and occupied. Old slum dwellings of the tenants were purchased and razed. Roads were improved, a hospital was erected nearby, and a whole area, formerly considered blighted, was opened up for new development.

"But the story of friendliness which began in one living room," says Patrick J. Mullaney,* "cannot be summed up in

* *Interracial Review,* November, 1952.

terms of material benefits alone. Its spiritual values measured in improved human relations and the recognition of human rights are close to incalculable. Mrs. Grant's friends, so different from one another in creed, color, and calling, found among themselves a bond of unity with which they welded together a whole community in united action. They not only forestalled an explosive situation among neighbors, they gave them an opportunity to see that neighborliness has no relation to the accidents of color. They created an atmosphere and an area where whites and Negroes live together in a spirit which finds its expression in a sincere and simple phrase, 'the nicest neighbor I've ever known.'"